IN SPIRIT AND IN TRUTH

IN SPIRIT AND IN TRUTH

The Challenge of Discernment for Canadian Anglicans Today

Edited by

Catherine Sider Hamilton
Peter M. B. Robinson
George Sumner

REGENT COLLEGE PUBLISHING

Vancouver, British Columbia

Regent College Publishing
5800 University Boulevard, Vancouver, BC V6T 2E4 Canada
Web: www.regentpublishing.com
E-mail: info@regentpublishing.com

Views expressed in works published by Regent College Publishing are those of the author and do not necessarily represent the official position of Regent College (www.regent-college.edu).

Scripture taken from the Holy Bible, New International Version®, unless otherwise noted. NIV® Copyright © 1973, 1978, 1984 by International Bible Society. Used by permission of Zondervan Publishing House. All rights reserved. Scripture quotations marked (KJV) are taken from the King James Version.

Library and Archives Canada Cataloguing in Publication Data

In spirit and in truth : the challenge of discernment for Canadian
Anglicans today / edited by Catherine Sider Hamilton,
George Sumner and Peter Robinson.

Includes bibliographical references.
ISBN 978-1-57383-443-8

1. Anglican Church of Canada—Doctrines. 2. Christian life—Anglican
authors. I. Hamilton, Catherine Sider II. Sumner, George R., 1955–
III. Robinson, Peter, 1962–

BX5615.A1I5 2009   230'.3   C2009-903338-0

Contents

Preface

I t is often said that Anglican theology has historically had a particularly occasional nature; one thinks readily of Richard Hooker and *The Laws* as an irenic response to a polemical situation in the writing of which decisive work on Anglican ecclesiology was accomplished. The following collection of essays is offered similarly in a time of great debate within the Anglican Communion about the proper teaching on human sexuality. As we have sought to dig down deeper to address this question, we hope that we have discovered some things of use about the nature of doctrine, authority, and the theological evaluation of the human person. It is the proper role of a faculty of theology to encourage and contribute to such work, and so I am happy to offer Wycliffe's support to this intellectual effort on behalf of the gospel in, I hope, a Hookerian irenic mode.

Real theology is always *pro ecclesia*, and so this project was conceived when we heard that the Primate's Theological Commission was welcoming contributions more widely as they addressed questions about development and the work of the Spirit in history in connection with their mandate from the General Synod of the Anglican Church of Canada, 2007. It is our hope that these essays will serve to foster further dialogue on these important subjects, and will make a contribution to the theological and spiritual welfare of the church of which we are servants. We are grateful for the encouragement and help of Regent Publishing to make these essays available.

George Sumner
Wycliffe College, Toronto
Feast of the Ascension, 2008

Introduction

This collection of essays responds to the invitation to the church issued by the Primate of the Anglican Church of Canada to reflect on two questions posed by General Synod 2007 in relation to same-sex blessings. These questions are:

The theological question whether the blessing of same-sex unions is a faithful, Spirit-led development of Christian doctrine;

Scripture's witness to the integrity of every human person and the question of the sanctity of human relationships.

These are rich questions, full of terms of real theological significance: "Spirit-led," "development of doctrine," "integrity," "sanctity." That the question about the faithfulness of same-sex blessings has been posed with such seriousness is commendable, even exciting. It opens up for the church an opportunity to grapple with aspects of Christian belief and practice that are fundamental, yet often go unexamined. What do we mean by "Spirit-led"? How might we recognize a decision that is "Spirit-led"? How do we measure a "faithful" development of doctrine? What is "integrity of the human person," and in what way might

Scripture be said to "witness" to it? Again, how do we identify "sanctity" and in what sense might human relationships be said, in Scripture, to have "sanctity"? The Primate's questions suggest both that these are important matters, and that some understanding of and consensus about the meaning of these terms is necessary before any decision can be made about the "faithfulness" of blessing same-sex unions.

The contributors to this volume—all Anglicans and scholars deeply engaged in the life of the church—seek to grant the questions their full seriousness, in the hope that the sustained reflection which they offer in these essays will be of service to the church in its deliberations about same-sex blessings, and more broadly in its continued growth and life as the people of God. Two essays, one by George Sumner and one by Christopher Seitz, consider the question of doctrine, its development and its relation to Scripture, Sumner in conversation with J. H. Newman and Seitz in relation to the revisionist argument from Acts 15. Robert Sears pleads for a sustained examination of the nature of doctrine and doctrinal change, offering to that end a typology of doctrine within which such change can be coherently addressed. Ephraim Radner, Robert Sider and Ron Kydd reflect on the meaning of "Spirit-led" through the lens of Scripture (especially the Gospel of John) and the writings of several early fathers of the church. In different ways all three point to the Christ-shaped character (as that shape is revealed in Scripture) of that which is Spirit-led. Three essays consider the intersection of church and culture in this debate: Roseanne Kydd looks at the way the meaning of words may shift under both grammatical and cultural pressure; George Egerton traces the influence of the secular human rights debates on the church's debate about same-sex blessings, and Grant LeMarquand addresses the issue of cultural readings of Scripture in a multi-cultural church.

In regard to the second of the Primate's questions, Dean Mercer asks about the meaning of an appeal to "Scripture's witness" in a debate that has seen a variety of approaches to Scripture, approaches that are, he argues, contradictory. Peter Robinson considers the meaning of "integrity" from the perspective of "image of God" theology and

Ian Henderson explores the terms "integrity" and "sanctity of relationships" in relation to biblical covenant theology. Catherine Hamilton traces several biblical readings of Genesis 3 in relation to the idea of the sanctity of human relationships and Lisa Wang, finally, offers a moving meditation on the meaning of sanctity, illuminated by voices from the New Testament and early church.

The essays represent a wide range of perspectives from which one might approach the questions that confront the church: the interpretive traditions of the biblical writers; the writings of the church fathers; J. H. Newman's reflection on doctrine; the tradition of Christian theological reflection more broadly; cultural and linguistic studies. In this diversity, however, a striking common theme emerges. All the essays, in one way or another, offer a particular "way of seeing," an approach to the current crisis—and to the church's decision-making generally—that is both catholic and evangelical. It is catholic in its instinct for the whole sweep of the Christian community throughout history and throughout the world. Paul and Susanna, Tertullian and Chrysostom, J. H. Newman and J. D. G. Dunn have, our authors suggest, something to say to us in our current deliberations; likewise, contemporary African Anglican readings of Scripture raise their voices in concert with Canadian and Peruvian and European readings to create a Christian community of interpretation within which we understand the meaning of Scripture, and God's purpose, for each moment in the church's life. These essays begin from the premise that the perspectives both of our forebears in the faith and of the world-wide church belong to our own perspective. The apostles' and church mothers' and fathers' ways of reading the Bible shape our ways of reading now; J. H. Newman's understanding of doctrine illuminates the meaning of doctrine for us now. Truth, the meaning of Scripture, the leading of the Spirit, may now be seen only in part in the Christian community insofar as it is human, but insofar as the Christian community properly seeks truth and the meaning of Scripture and the leading of the Spirit, it seeks them in conversation with, and in the same ways as, its ancestors and fellow-travelers in the faith. Its way of seeing, its way of reading Scripture and truth, follows from theirs.

What then is characteristic of the Christian community's way of reading? These essays point to several things. First, an acceptance of Scripture as a formative text: by this narrative, by this history, by this prophecy and teaching and apocalyptic hope the Christian community shall be shaped. Scripture's story is the story we accept as the truth about the world: it is what is real.

Second, when there is debate about the meaning of Scripture or the shape of what is true and right, the community is not free to jettison Scripture, or even those parts of it that offend. The essays all insist on working through Scripture, and treating it as a unified whole. Genesis and Revelation stand as beginning and end of a vast edifice in which narrative, poetry, prophecy and prayer are woven together to reveal something of the mystery of God and God's purpose for the world. All of it, from Genesis to Revelation, from Amos to Paul and Job to 1 John is necessary to the meaning of the mystery.

Thirdly, the reading of Scripture (and so judgments about truth and right) coincides, these essays suggest, with the doctrinal and conciliar life of the church. Scripture and its meaning leads in a conciliar process to teaching about the church's ordering of faith and life; doctrine likewise serves as a reference point for the understanding of Scripture. Creed and ethics, Scripture and statements of faith, thus are intertwined. Neither Scripture nor doctrine, neither ethics nor creed, stands alone.

And finally, the reading of Scripture in the Christian community, as these essays reflect it, is both a broad one and bounded. It is broad in its sweep, encompassing as it does interpretations from Paul to Rowan Williams, from first century Rome to twenty-first century Kenya. It is bounded in the requirement for coherence: Scripture interprets but does not contradict Scripture; so, too, the church's reading from beginning to end. In this sense the central interpretive impulse is cath-olic—grounded in the whole witness of the church throughout history; and evangelical—grounded in Scripture first of all.

These essays illustrate in various ways this catholic and evangelical approach to the church's reading: reading truth, reading the times; in both, reading Scripture. We offer them as an articulation of the presuppositions by which we may move forward in a time of serious disagreement, and in the belief that their approach, at once catholic and evangelical, rooted in Scripture and in the community of the faithful, captures the peculiar genius of Anglicanism and, more broadly, something of what it means to be the church.

Catherine Sider Hamilton
Pentecost, 2008

Contributors

George Egerton
Associate Professor of History, Emeritus
University of British Columbia
Vancouver, British Columbia, Canada

Catherine Sider Hamilton
Doctoral candidate and Instructor in New Testament Greek
Wycliffe College;
Honorary Assistant, Grace Church on-the-Hill
Toronto, Ontario, Canada

Ian H. Henderson
Associate Professor of New Testament and Early Christianity
Faculty of Religious Studies
McGill University
Montreal, Quebec, Canada

Ronald A. N. Kydd
Research Professor of Church History
Tyndale Seminary
Toronto, Ontario, Canada

Roseanne Kydd
Music Minister, St. Philip's on-the-Hill
Unionville, Ontario, Canada

Grant LeMarquand
Academic Dean and Associate Professor of Biblical Studies and Mission
Trinity School for Ministry
Ambidge, Pennsylvania, U.S.A.

F. Dean Mercer
Incumbent, St. Paul's L'Amoreaux;
Adjunct Professor of Liturgics
Wycliffe College
Toronto, Ontario, Canada

Ephraim Radner
Professor of Historical Theology
Wycliffe College
Toronto, Ontario, Canada

Peter M. B. Robinson
Incumbent, Emmanuel Church, Richvale;
Adjunct Professor of Theology
Wycliffe College
Toronto, Ontario, Canada

Christopher Seitz
Research Professor of Biblical Interpretation
Wycliffe College
Toronto, Ontario, Canada

Robert Sears
Incumbent, Parish of Chelsea, Lascelles, Wakefield
Diocese of Ottawa, Ontario, Canada

Robert D. Sider
Charles E. Dana Professor Emeritus of Classical Languages
Dickinson College
Carlisle, Pennsylvania, U.S.A.

George Sumner
Principal and Helliwell Professor of World Mission
Wycliffe College
Toronto, Ontario, Canada

Lisa Wang
Associate Priest, The Cathedral Church of St. James
Toronto, Ontario, Canada

On Doctrine

CHAPTER ONE

What Would John Henry Newman Do?

George Sumner

The genesis of the present volume may be found in the effort, stemming from a mandate of the General Synod of the Anglican Church of Canada, to consider whether or not the blessing of same-sex unions is a development of doctrine. A new approach is a welcome one for several reasons. Church people on both sides of the issue often sense that they are speaking past one another. The synod itself in its debate and aftermath swirled around terms like "core doctrine" and "adiaphoron," the vagueness of whose use did not conduce to logical precision, to say the least.[1] But the claim of this article is stronger: this particular new approach holds out special promise. First of all, addressing the question in this way allows us to bring this vexed question into relation with a serious tradition of theological reflection related to Anglicanism and cognizant of the problems of modern historical criticism. In other words, there has been a theological tool in the shed for this job we have heretofore overlooked. Secondly, the most famous example of the literature on development offers a proposal for criteria to identify a development, and the work for this reason deserves our consideration. For after the squabbling over the possibility of a development is finished, we are left precisely with the question of criteria: is the case before us a development, and how would we know? Thirdly, posing the same-sex-union question in terms of development by its very nature will imagine in a broader way who the proper jury, and what the relevant evidence, for such a verdict would be. To the demonstration of these three points we now move.

To be sure, these reasons for encouragement may not coincide with the hopes some may harbor for the development-tack. It may be that the word itself summons up for some an optimistic view of the evolution of our own culture toward greater spiritual enlightenment, a hoped-for coincidence between cultural trend and movement of Spirit which is a distinguishing trait of liberal theology. One may on this score think of the fondness Presiding Bishop Frank Griswold of the Episcopal Church U.S.A. had for the verses in John 16 about the truths the Holy Spirit had not yet led us into. It may even be, at some level conscious or unconscious, that a certain coincidence between developed doctrine and the "developed" world, at least on the issue of sexuality, is imagined. But as we shall see, this warm feeling for "development" is hardly borne out by a closer consideration of its intellectual requirements.

Before we set to work, however, a bit more clearing of the brush of common misunderstandings of the idea of "development" itself is in order. Consider the following quotation from a theologian of the Anglican Church of Canada on the contemporary question of development: "the Nicene Creed uses a new (non-Biblical!) word to speak of the relation between the Father and the Son, because the Bible is not an adequate resource to solve the problem. It does not quite say what the church wants to say."[2] We are left with the impression that Athanasius knows more than Paul, and we know rather more still. To be sure, the *homoousios*, "of one being," is the prime example of a development of doctrine. But it is classic not because the Bible was "not an adequate resource," but precisely because, in a new circumstance, this neologism borrowed from Greek philosophical parlance allowed the church to sum up in one word the Bible's central insight, namely that Jesus was Lord.[3]

In other words, *homoousios* is the classic example of a legitimate development of doctrine because it uses new language to answer a new question, namely the metaphysical nature of the relation of the first two persons of the Trinity, but this "new" thought grows out of, and gives concise expression to what we find Paul and John saying about the relation of Father and Son. Development in this case can be captured neither by "say the same thing" nor "say something new and unknown."

From this example, properly understood, we learn several key things about development. First of all, the consideration of doctrine must not be seen as an end-run around Scripture. On the contrary, here as elsewhere, doctrine, growing from Scripture, serves to guide our reading of Scripture.[4] Secondly, a development is not simply some new fact we did not know before, a "z," to be added to claims w, x, and y which we were already making. Rather, z, if it is to be a development, must be an insight which, in a new circumstance, allows w, x, y, and z to say what w, x, and y said before. In this way, the doctrine under consideration as a development cannot be studied in isolation, but needs to be thought about in relation to the larger doctrinal claim made to date by the tradition.

As the example of the *homoousios* clearly shows, the question of development has endured throughout Christian history; it is endemic to a faith in the One who is "the same yesterday, today, and forever,"[5] yet whose people journey through eras and cultures. But the question as it is found in the tradition of thought we are interested in derives from the modern period in particular. For it is born of the anxiety of historical consciousness which is a trademark of modernity.[6] And as such it is well equipped to address our present debate, behind which lurks a kind of unbridled contextualism, for which teachings would be made specific to settings in order to serve the purposes of each setting. By contrast, to espouse a development of doctrine is precisely to discern amidst historical change an enduring claim, continuity amidst changes.

For us as Anglicans the classic text on the subject, though in some ways an ironic one, is John Henry Newman's *An Essay in Aid of a Doctrine of the Development of Doctrine*. Newman was of course one of the sparks of the Oxford Movement, the great Anglican defender of the *via media*, "the middle way," between Rome and Geneva. Doctrinally, this position entailed a defense of the unchanging deposit of the first five centuries. Yet by the 1840s Newman had come to see that new questions had arisen, and old questions asked in new ways, and that, as the *homoousios* question itself shows, immobility might come to entail error as well as truth. This questioning led eventually to his conversion to Roman Catholicism, and to the writing of his book about development. The irony is of course that it was as a Catholic that he wrote the book, and that the doctrine of development appealed in part because he was convinced that without the strong magisterium implied therein Protestantism would, under cultural pressures, drift afield!

Newman would surely not have claimed that he could offer a proof that a particular proposal was in fact a true development of doctrine. But he offers a series of "tests," of criteria, which cumulatively could give a sense of the plausibility of a claim of development. I want to highlight three criteria, which are representative of the whole list and decisive in the case before us. First of all, Newman talked about "preservation of type": across different settings, expressed in different terms, does the idea maintain its shape and meaning across a variety of what we would call "contexts"? It is at just this point that the missiological implications, the cash-out for the conduct of the Christian mission, are clearest. For one of the gifts of a worldwide, i.e. catholic, understanding of mission, is that one corner of the global church can correct or advise another: is the tack you are taking true to the faith once delivered, and what will be the implications of its pursuit?[7] Is a proposal a valid adaptation of a biblical insight to a local setting, or is it an example of local factors overtaking and obscuring the gospel? We all may say we want to be a missional church, or to "move from maintenance to mission," but what if this were to involve a willingness to listen to voices that tell us things we are not accustomed to hearing?

Paired with this may be found "chronic endurance," which denotes the idea's sheer power to persist as a cogent proposal across time. Taken together they bespeak the kind of patience that is required for the discernment of a development. They also show us the breadth and scope of vision that is needed for such a judgment. One must look at a wider cross-section of churches and eras than we might suppose. The question must be recast as one for the church catholic, one involving generations before and after, involving a wider ecumenical consultation.

The third test that is particularly pertinent to the case before us was named by Newman "early anticipation." It touches directly on the question of the relationship between doctrine and Scripture, for it states that a true development must have some germ to be found already in the witness of Scripture. There must be something in the biblical witness that in time grows into the doctrine itself, in contrast to a sheer *novum* with no preceding expression. One must be able to show a trajectory of thought, what Newman calls in another test "logical sequence," from those scriptural beginnings to the doctrine itself.

Our task is now to apply these criteria for development to the doctrine at hand: but what precisely is that doctrine? Well, the blessing of same-sex unions, of course. But one may swiftly note that traditional marriage has been understood as the blessing of a union. In other words, traditional marriage and same-sex unions are in this respect described in the same way. We can see that this proposal cannot be set apart as something other than a new kind of marriage, a new definition of marriage. Furthermore, the very heart of a marriage is the making of vows of lifelong fidelity before God, in the wake of which the blessing is pronounced. The vows are "performative," in the parlance of the philosophy of language, since their utterance changes the status of those involved. Unless the same-sex unions are not envisioned to be lifelong (which would present problems of its own), the very same heart of the rite would be found in the blessing of same-sex unions. In other words, as secular brothers and sisters are quick to recognize, the distinction between a union and a marriage lacks a difference.

So what then is the doctrine whose development is proposed? The answer is of course Christian marriage. And where are we to find this doctrine? Throughout Christian history, but for us as Anglicans, specifically in Canada, it is to be found in the marriage rite of the Book of

Common Prayer and the Book of Alternative Services, which continue to be the doctrinally definitive documents for our church.[8] The development in question is the revision of the doctrine of marriage as found in the Prayer Book to include same-sex couples. At the risk of belaboring the obvious, it may be pointed out that we are not talking about the introduction of a totally new doctrine, where nothing had existed before, but rather we are proposing the revision of an existing doctrine. And what do we find in our doctrine of marriage, in its unrevised state? Look at the wedding rite in the Prayer Book. The Exhortation cites the creation of the human in Genesis 1, which had the form of "male and female," who then yearn for their joining. The wedding at Cana in John 2, and Paul's meditation on the spiritual meaning of the marriage of man and woman in Ephesians 5, add to this relationship rooted in the creative intention of God an additional meaning in the new dispensation having to do with the bond between nothing less than Christ and the church. This linking of divine intention in the order of creation and in the order of salvation is of great importance.[9] God wills the creation in a particular form, and it is this very creation, in spite of its deformation in sin, which he wills to save through the work of Christ. The New Testament's specific references to the marriage of male and female, then, stand as a crucial "outward and visible sign" for human being of God's gracious intention at the very juncture of creation and redemption.[10]

The lections for the nuptial mass go on to cite Mark 10, where Jesus himself says that since God created the human male and female from the foundation of creation (in a citation of Genesis 1), they are to be joined together in marriage (a reference to the "cleaving" in Genesis 2). This theme of the intention of creation is reinforced by procreation as an aim of matrimony, in keeping with the exhortation also in Genesis 1 to be "fruitful and multiply." The theme of procreation also offers one dimension of the meaning of the *imago Dei* in Genesis 1:26, since the male and the female, different from and communicating with one another, procreate new life as an expression of their love and stewardship.[11]

Let us pause here for a moment. First of all we must note that the rite itself, through multiple scriptural citations, defines marriage to be between man and woman.[12] Revisionists at times contend that opposition to same-sex unions stems from literalistic biblical proof-texting. But this is hardly the case. The definition of marriage as a relationship between a man and a woman is based on a word of Jesus, which is built in turn on the doctrine of creation itself, a major pillar of theology as a whole. It is bolstered by multiple words from Paul. Thus we have a doctrine of marriage of the male and the female on the strongest authority.[13] And so to revisionists who may ask why traditionalists oppose same-sex marriages in and of themselves, the answer is because of what we are for, the marriage of man and woman, and why we are for it, its multiple scriptural warrant and close relation to central doctrines of the faith.[14]

The doctrine is marriage, and the key criteria are preservation of type, chronic endurance, and early anticipation. Before we move to application, it is important to note that a successful candidate needs to pass all the hurdles, not just one. For this reason the church intends that success should be hard and slow, in order that the church might be sure that it does not corrupt the doctrinal inheritance which it is the particular responsibility of bishops to protect. As is so often true in critical testing of any kind, as one finds for example in science, falsification is easier than verification. So it is with the case before us as well: failing even one of the tests should bring a halt to the proposed revision, at least for the present.

And how does this revision fare as a proposed development of the doctrine of marriage? Not well. First of all, let us consider the consultation across cultural lines and ecumenical considerations which are entailed in preservation of type. Anglican theological leaders in most parts of the world do not recognize this as a valid development. The major denominations that make up most of the world's Christians, the Roman Catholics, the Orthodox, the Pentecostals, and various evangelicals, are a united chorus in opposition. In fact pursuing this course will seriously damage those relationships. What could be clearer evidence of a failure to pass the "preservation of type" test? With respect to chronic endurance, we should recall that, while the traditional view has been the consensus for almost twenty centuries, the revised view has only been found among a relatively small number of Christians for two generations. Does this mean that the proposal could never pass these tests? No, but it does mean that it manifestly has not done so yet.

With respect to early anticipation, the evidence is equally discouraging. We are dealing with an issue about which the relevant passages of Scripture are all negative. We cannot point to passages moving in contrary directions, as we can in the case of the ordination of women, for example, about the relation between which we may ask questions. And Scripture's negative account touches, as we have seen, on many of the great doctrines of the church. In sum, when we look at the question, with the aid of Newman's criteria for the development of doctrine, in a broader light, neither the scope of cultures, nor of eras, nor of Scriptures, gives us any encouragement to proceed now with such an innovation.

The main point of this paper has been that asking the same-sex-union question in relation to development has promise. We have concluded that such an approach offers no evidence of support for such a revision. Over this question we as a church have already gone through a period of protracted conflict and pain, with more surely to come. We are not criticizing the raising and debating of the question. The Anglican tradition at its best has been as open to theological speculation as it has been conservative about doctrinal change. Nor should we be despondent about these struggles vis-à-vis the question of development in particular. It has been precisely through this crisis that the instruments of unity have come into the spotlight, and are haltingly become serviceable. They are potentially just the kind of conciliar forms to provide the testing, the sober spiritual second thoughts, that a sound theory of development requires. Development is not a reason to move ahead on one's own: it drives us back to the constraints of communion!

"And so we do not lose heart."[15] For it would be wrong amidst all the questions to lose sight of the great promise held by the steps which the

Anglican Communion has taken forward as a result of this conflict. As we have seen, John Henry Newman could not find in Anglicanism structures sufficient to maintain the integrity of the faith amidst the challenges of proposed novel doctrines. But Newman could not have imagined an Anglicanism that was truly global. It turns out that the Communion itself provides for us the means to implement the tests across time and culture which he proposes. We need to pray that the communion's fabric will remain sufficiently intact for these not-so-new means of testing developments of doctrine to work.

NOTES

1. A186 passed due to the reassuring rider that "not-inconsistent with core doctrine" meant simply that such unions are not "creedal." In itself this claim of non-inconsistency implies nothing about the claim's truth. But after the passage of the motion assorted prelates and chancellors have stated that theological impediments to passage are now removed. It is hard to know where the illogical ends and the disingenuous begins.

2. The Rev. William Harrison in the *Anglican Journal*, April 2008, p. 6.

3. Such is the main point of Rowan Williams; magisterial *Arius: Heresy and Tradition* (Grand Rapids: Eerdmans, 2002).

4. Here we should add that surely the initial qualifying test for a development is that it not contradict "the Word of God written" in its plain sense. So Hooker would have claimed. On this basis the case for same-sex unions founders at the outset. Still, the debate as it is being conducted is worth consideration.

5. Heb 13:8.

6. See Owen Chadwick, *From Bossuet to Newman: The Idea of Doctrinal Development* (Cambridge: Cambridge University Press, 1987).

7. A good example of this may be found in Lesslie Newbigin's *The Gospel in a Pluralist Society* (London: SPCK, 1989).

8. It is sometimes claimed that our Church is distinguished by not having doctrines of our own, but as Stephen Sykes so eloquently argues in *The Integrity of Anglicanism* (Oxford: Mowbrays, 1978), our prayer book tradition entails a number of doctrines, of which the present doctrine would be one. Surely the fondness for the patristic maxim *lex orandi lex credendi* only reinforces this conclusion.

9. The severing of creation and redemption was at the heart of the Gnostic heresy, to which moderns, with their own kind of dualisms, are particularly prone.

10. I was helped on this point by our editor, Catherine Hamilton.

11. It is mistaken ethical thinking to suppose that relations which are exceptions, such as older or sterile couples, disprove the point about the shape of the relations. The Roman Catholic church is surely right at least in this much, that the capacity to bear children is normative for marital relations of a man and a woman. Nor should the liturgical revision to elevate other aims along with procreation in the BAS be taken to mean the removal of this aim.

12. For this reason a mere addition of a canon cannot suffice to change marriage; one would have to change the words of Jesus found in the Gospel and quoted by the rite itself!

13. By contrast we may note that Rom 1:26's opposition is based precisely in the form of the relationship, male with male and female with female, which shows the element of disorder indicative of the disruption of sin of which we all partake. So arguments that describe the point of the passage as a rejection of the abusive nature of the particular relations described cannot be correct.

14. This was precisely the point of the St. Michael Report, namely that this is a doctrine, and though not a "core doctrine," yet it is one that is intimately linked to central doctrines of the faith. To conclude, as Synod did, that as a result one could be free to change the doctrine because it is not "core" is to stand the report's point on its head.

15. 2 Cor 4:1

CHAPTER TWO

Scripture and Doctrine in the St. Michael Report

A Reflection on Scripture and Theology in the Canadian Anglican Context

Christopher Seitz

THE RELATIONSHIP BETWEEN SCRIPTURE AND DOCTRINE

Why has an appeal to "doctrine" apparently replaced, or now stands in for, the first-order appeal to Scripture more customarily undertaken when the report examines the issue of same-sex blessings? Because no explanation for the prioritizing of "doctrine" as a category of its own is given (we leave to the side the passing comments that Scripture exists in its liturgical presentation; or that Scripture is only "doctrine in the making"), one is left to presume. It bears reflection that for a central Anglican thinker like Hooker, even if one chose to pay particular attention to his use of "reason" in relation to Scripture (over against appeal to the church, as in Roman Catholic approaches, in respect of Scripture's authority; or over against something like "self-authenticating authority" with elements of Reformed thought) it remains incontrovertible that within his frame of reference theological statements proceed from scriptural reflection in some form.[1] It is not possible to speak of "doctrine" apart from the sentences, paragraphs, and larger canonical form of the church's Scriptures. Why has the situation changed in the context of our present Anglican struggles?

It is important to reflect on this development, for even if the matter is assessed without the proper proportion, or a wrong explanation is provided, it remains the case that the way Scripture has ceased functioning as the chief ground of appeal calls for specific comment. This is all the more true because it would be a curious development if doctrine could somehow become a replacement for Scripture, which is the foundation of its very logic and force. In his battle with the Arians over "of one substance" Athanasius engaged in page after page of exegetical argument from Proverbs 8. There was no doctrinal point to be made that was anything less, so far as he was concerned, than Scripture coming to its proper boil—recourse to "creeds" or "doctrine" would have begged the question precisely under debate. Scripture was not for him texts familiar from liturgical presentation, nor was it even the New Testament's take on the history of Israel's religion in the Old Testament, but rather entailed a sustained exegetical probing of the plain sense of an Old Testament text (Proverbs 8) so as to hear its Christian voice in respect of creation, God Almighty, and the Son. Just how were these central matters and figures related? Examples from the ante-Nicene fathers would make the point even clearer: there the Rule of Faith is a drawing out of the Christological heart of the Scriptures the church inherited from the Jews, in relationship to the growing testimony of what would in time become the second testament of Christian Scripture. Precisely when there are no formal creeds, and no formal "doctrine," Scripture does its first-order work. As with the example of Athanasius, that does not change in the subsequent life of the church, but becomes all the more the case, precisely when creedal confession is under pressure or in need of clarification.

One explanation for this recent alternative is that the appeal to "doctrine" sets up the possibility that "doctrine" is more amenable to progression, development, and change, and therein lies the rationale for referring to it, rather than Scripture. It serves better the larger purpose of the movement for change in the church's understanding of marriage. This notion probably has its roots in the idea that Scripture too changes, or progresses, from weaker to stronger kinds of claims on the Christian church, given its two-testament character. This notion has deep roots in late-eighteenth and nineteenth century assumptions about the nature of historical change, and an assessment of the two testaments of the one canon of Scripture made on the basis of this, at least in the intellectual West. It does not conform to the longstanding concern in the catholic church for the ontological claims of Scripture (that the triune God is at work in creation, in Israel, in promise and in reality); the Old speaking of Christ in its idiom, the New in its idiom. Or in Augustine's famous expression, Jesus Christ is in the Old Testament *latent*, in the New Testament *patent*.

This hunch is confirmed by the presence of a single, persistent appeal to one scriptural text in the otherwise untidy and parlous landscape of reflections on Scripture in the sexuality debates. One should note that these debates began by challenging assumptions about the plain sense of individual texts traditionally seen to be significant in the way Christians thought about sexuality (Leviticus, Romans, Paul's letters to the Corinthians). We leave to the side here whether such individual texts only ever made sense against a much thicker account of sexuality based upon comprehensive accounts of the nature of creation, Israel as bride, covenant relationships as based in love, the church as bride of Christ, and so forth. The point to be made is that appeal to individual texts as requiring a fresh reassessment has shifted over the years.[2] This is in part due to the fact that even "liberal" readers of Scripture agreed that these individual texts did say what they had traditionally been held to say, and that therefore the Bible really needed to be placed under a more inventive or severe kind of appraisal: it was simply outdated, wrong, or culturally constrained. This is a different line of argument, and so requires, theologically, some defense of a quasi-doctrinal and non-exegetical nature (the "spirit's new word"). Here is the Scripture/doctrine cleavage manifesting itself.

In the wake of this, how might one then think about the role of Scripture? This question became acute once the ground was cut out from under the "it is possible to read these texts in some other way" idea, precisely for those wishing to claim the Bible really was a good or serviceable book after all and not to be rejected. Post-modernity in some forms came to the aid as an ally, by arguing that "plain sense" or "thick accounts" were themselves constructs, and that texts cannot have the kind of constructive and constraining force Christians have more traditionally taken them to have. The appeal to individual proof texts was stalled altogether by a larger notion that the Bible really cannot deliver something like a plain or constraining sense. At best it instantiates religious motives, or points to ideals or virtues of various kinds. One sees something of this kind of use of Scripture in the St. Michael Report.

THE APPEAL TO ACTS 15 IN THE PRESENT DISCUSSION

The text that has weathered the debates and continues to be appealed to in many circles is Acts 15.[3] One thesis of the present essay is that the appeal to Acts 15 explains why doctrine has become a detachable category, out beyond the traditional appeals to the plain sense of Scripture.

Acts 15 records the adjudication of the decision of Peter to baptize a gentile believer. Attractive here is the notion that Acts 15 speaks of something like "the first council of the church." On that ground, it serves to provide an analogy to our present discussions, outside the framework of Acts, the New Testament, and Christian Scripture as a whole. The church is now facing a moment of adjudication like the apostolic decision-making event that takes place within the New Testament.

Secondly, Acts 15 is thought to be useful because religious convictions said to be operative in the past are here, it is argued, being set aside. As that was true then, so it is true now. Acts 15 saw the setting aside of older revelation, and we need to set aside older catholic and scriptural teaching on human sexuality.

Thirdly, Acts 15 records that the Holy Spirit was at work in the early decisions of Peter and of the decision-making body in Jerusalem. The Holy Spirit is that agent who declares older teaching to be in need of revamping and, if need be, overturning. The Holy Spirit is the warrant for moving beyond scriptural or catholic teaching, and for addressing a new day with a "new truth."

Several things can be said about the appropriateness of these three points, and of others that may be said to follow from them. First, it is unclear in general terms whether the church in the late modern West may be free to think of itself as on direct analogy with the apostolic community of the New Testament, and this for several key reasons. The church of the late modern West is divided, and so the claims of one of its number (The Anglican Church of Canada) to be "the Church" are themselves part of the cause of the problems we now must face. The fact that other churches (including the vast majority of Christians today and through time) have reached a clear decision about the matter in question, and base this on either Scripture or received tradition or both, establishes the point.

Further, the apostolic community of the book of Acts is facing a problem which in the very nature of the case is an internal New Testament one, and not easily related to the post-biblical church (however we define its scope and character). That is, how is the Jewish Christian body of apostles properly to reflect on an issue involving the extension of the gospel into a gentile world? The ruling itself shows that the decision was made precisely as an address to this issue: the gentiles were to be seen as sojourners in Israel, and so those proscriptions that applied to them in the law of Moses (Leviticus 17 and 18) would here be operative. The very fact that the Western text of Acts has a different set of proscriptions reveals at once that the analogy was imperfect once the Christian church became largely severed from its Jewish roots, roots which are everywhere in place in Acts and in the apostolic circle which declared Israel's Messiah Lord and God. This problem (of a Jewish

Christian church seeking to bring gentiles into its fellowship in a manner consistent with prophets and the Holy Spirit and the dominical teaching) is manifestly not the problem of late modern decisions about same-sex blessings.

Then there is the related problem, moving to the second point, that the ruling given in Acts 15 overthrows nothing at all. It is seen to be consistent with the prophets. Indeed, as has been shown without a doubt, the ruling is based upon the law of Moses, and derives its logic from Leviticus's understanding of the sojourner in the midst of Israel.[4] All in the council agree. The Old Testament spoke, did it not, of the gospel breaking forth from its own covenantal logic? That question would surely have been answered "Yes" by all involved in the decision. At question was precisely not overthrowing, but upholding the Law and the Prophets. Again, there was no possibility of "doctrine" being anything other than an appeal to the Scriptures—an appeal in no way hindered because those in the New Testament had no New Testament, it might be added.

Finally, (in regard to the third point), the Holy Spirit's work, we are told by Peter, was to bring to mind what the Lord Jesus had said. This simply confirms the larger logic already rehearsed. The Holy Spirit "spake by the prophets" (as the later creeds would put it, based on texts like these and on the presentation of the Old Testament itself.) The Holy Spirit spake in relationship to the dominical teaching remembered. The Holy Spirit spake through Scripture and Lord to confirm to all the decision reached. We leave to the side whether Acts 15 was ever very useful given that its proscriptions could be said to be anything but "liberalizations" in respect of the sexual conduct now expected of sojourners baptized in the name of Jesus, insofar as the consistent witness of Acts 15 (in the Western text as well) was prohibition of *porneia*. In the early church this meant the classical understanding of Christian marriage as the sole context for sexual activity.

CONCLUSIONS

The late modern appeal to doctrine, with its attendant notion of "Holy Spirit overturning," has treated the Bible in such a way that it searches for moments of direct analogy and then applies them, in this way assuming that Scripture's authority has been retained in important ways. An event inside of Scripture itself becomes a "doctrinal moment" capable of standing alone, in this way showing the church to be like what it seeks to find. This demands of course a serious commitment to individual texts and discrete episodes (read according to what George Lindbeck calls an experiential-expressivist hermeneutic), and not to the comprehensive scope of Scripture, which inheres with its claim to be Scripture, and not discrete episodes in religious history.[5]

Here we also see why the report will incline toward saying Holy Scripture "contains" things. That verb of course was deployed in Anglican and more generally Christian circles long before the advent of what Lindbeck classified as the experiential-expressivist handling of Scripture, itself an outgrowth of nineteenth-century notions of history and biblical reference. By using this traditional word in a context very different than its original usage (there is a pattern developing here), the Holy Scriptures are turned into episodes of decision-making and "doctrinal," spirit-led, reconsiderations. One need only consider that the idea of "containing all things necessary to salvation" sat closely in Anglican articles alongside the idea of Scripture "not being expounded in such wise that one portion be repugnant to another." Both are consistent with the spirit of Cranmer's collect, whereby "God Almighty has caused all Holy Scriptures to be written for our learning." The ideas of selectivity or evolving religious history were not key conceptualities in the framework of earliest Anglican Christian theology.

The central role given to "doctrine" follows of course from developments in other parts of the liberal Anglican West, along with its stepchild "core doctrine." One can see almost immediately how far removed this notion of a separation of "doctrine" from Scripture is from either the Rule of Faith or the baptismal interrogatories of earliest Christianity, or the actual creeds themselves. The exegetical pressure exerting itself in each of these instances is enormous. In modernity this close association of Scripture and doctrine could only be ignored by turning the Bible into an altogether different version of the Reformation's *sola scriptura*: that is, detaching it from its organic relationship to catholic teaching in the form of creeds and the Rule of Faith (the word is of course the same one used of canons of Scripture), and then creating a "core doctrine" because in the meantime the notion of theological or doctrinal address, in a full sense, had lost its logic and durability detached from comprehensive scriptural moorings. What was left to do, then, was to seize on a text like Acts 15 and say it was offering some warrant for commitments already well underway to full prosecution anyway. It became a doctrinally charged "for instance" from antiquity of modern efforts to introduce change and claim for the changes some loose biblical and theological warrant.

Ironically, this is its own form of selective proof-texting. This is a handling of the Bible said by progressives to be the problem in traditional appeals to texts in defense of Christian marriage and against the blessing of same-sex behavior, and yet in reality, it has its own acute form in most progressive appeals to changing the scriptural and theological teaching. In a debate such as this, it is important to understand how Scripture and doctrine reinforce and inform one another, as this has consistently been maintained in classical Anglican and catholic sources.

ENDNOTES

1 See the recent treatment of Nigel Voak, "Richard Hooker and the Principle of Sola Scriptura," *Journal of Theological Studies* 59 (2008): 177–96. Voak, who argues for a vigorous and innovative appeal to reason on Hooker's part, nevertheless accepts that this is a hermeneutical appeal in conjunction with Scripture and that Scripture's central role is undiminished. Indeed, Hooker likely thought this appeal best brought out Scripture's theological word to the church. (The debate is a technical one having to do with Hooker's bearing toward and dependency on classical Reformed thought of the period, or a Roman Catholic alternative, itself undergoing change).

2 Christopher Seitz, "Sexuality and Scripture's Plain Sense: The Christian Community and the Law of God," in *Homosexuality, Science and the "Plain Sense" of Scripture* (ed. David Balch; Grand Rapids: Eerdmans, 2000), 177–96.

3 For an early popular account, see Luke Timothy Johnson, *Decision-Making in the Church: A Biblical Model* (Philadelphia: Fortress Press, 1983).

4 Richard Bauckham, "James and the Gentiles (Acts 15:13–21)," in *History, Literature, and Society in the Book of Acts* (ed. Ben Witherington, III; Cambridge: Cambridge University Press, 1996), 154–84. My own treatment of Acts 15 is "Dispirited: Scripture as Rule of Faith and Recent Misuse of the Council of Jerusalem," in *Figured Out* (Louisville: Westminster John Knox, 2001), 117–29.

5 George Lindbeck, *The Nature of Doctrine: Religion and Theology in a Postliberal Age* (Louisville: Westminster John Knox, 1984).

CHAPTER THREE

The Need for a
Typology of Doctrine

*Responsible Stewardship of Truth
and the Development of Doctrine*

Robert Sears

*The difficulties of a complicated faith are only the
reflection of the difficulties of a complicated life.*
—Henry Scott Holland

I s the blessing of same-sex unions a development of doctrine? This
is a theological question, and responsible theological stewardship
requires clear and intentional reflection and declaration concerning
both the nature of doctrine and the nature of doctrinal change. What
is needed, in the words of the St. Michael Report, is "a full theological
reflection" (§20).[1]

This essay argues that, without an explicit theory of the nature
of doctrine, our reflections at General Synod 2007 suffered. It also
argues that the St. Michael Report discusses the nature of doctrinal
development in what seem to be two incompatible ways; thus it seems
inadequate as the basis of our corporate reflections on doctrinal development, as it might conceivably lead us into contradictions though our
conclusions would seem to us to be clear.

In an effort to assist our corporate reflections on doctrine and doctrinal development, this essay offers a brief typology of the nature of doctrine. Four theories of doctrine are presented: rationalist, experientialist, culturalist, and realist. The rationalist and experientialist theories are most familiar, but the culturalist theory is operative in many contemporary theological discussions, including the St. Michael Report. I argue that only the realist theory of doctrine speaks to the question of the transcultural and transhistoric continuity of doctrine required for responsible development of doctrine. A typology of doctrine is invaluable to our response to a complex issue, enabling us to be clearer in our corporate reflections and more precise in our corporate declarations.

CORE DOCTRINE AND ADIAPHORA

For all the good work of the St. Michael Report, it does not explicitly address either the question of the nature of doctrine or the question of the nature of doctrinal development. The Report begins and concludes by recognizing the "range of interpretations given to the term 'doctrine'" (§§1, 8, 42), without ever specifying which one should guide our deliberations. How can the church be led in a full theological reflection about whether or not the blessing of same-sex unions is a development of doctrine (§44), when it is not clear which interpretation of doctrine we should be considering and what constitutes "development"?

The Report does offer a general summary of what doctrine is: "Doctrine is taken to refer generally to that teaching of the Church which is founded on Scripture, interpreted in the context of tradition, with the use of reason" (§8). The question arises whether introducing the "finer distinction" between "core doctrine" and *"adiaphora"* helps clarify matters sufficiently. At General Synod in 2007 we saw some confusion regarding Motion A186. After some amendments the motion came to read: "That this General Synod resolves that the blessing of same-sex unions is not in conflict with the core doctrine (in the sense of being creedal) of The Anglican Church of Canada."[2] On the surface this motion seemed to promise a welcome clarity in our conclusions. If one voted in favour of the motion, then this would be seen as believing that the blessing of same-sex unions would be permissible. If one voted against the motion, then it would be seen as not permissible. Unfortunately, this appearance was deceiving, because nothing concerning the morality or permissibility of the blessing of same-sex unions logically follows either from affirming or defeating this motion.

There are three reasons for this:

First, there is nothing said in the creeds about human sexuality. Marriage itself is not affirmed by them, so to say that the blessing of same-sex unions is not in conflict with the creeds is a red herring. Nothing follows from the claim that the blessing of same-sex unions is not in conflict with the creeds. The only thing added by the affirmation is the appearance of propriety in the conclusions that follow, since we all accept the creeds.

Second, there is an ambiguity in the specification of core doctrine as understood as, or in the sense of being, creedal doctrine. This could be understood as the unexceptionable claim that creedal doctrine is a necessary condition in defining core doctrine, i.e. no account of core doctrine could exclude the creeds. However, there is also a suggestion of a much bolder claim that creedal doctrine is not only a necessary condition of core doctrine, but also that it is a sufficient condition. That would mean that the creeds exhaustively define "core doctrine." This latter sense is problematic because, for example, core doctrine includes baptism, and personal transformation, not explicitly creedal, is nonetheless a part of baptismal teaching. Speaking of the early church, the BAS introduction to Holy Baptism states: "Becoming a Christian had as much to do with learning to live a new lifestyle within the Christian community as it did with specific beliefs" (BAS p. 146). Making this point, the 2008 Kuala Lumpur Report of The Third Inter-Anglican Theological and Doctrinal Commission wrote, "it is a serious mistake to think that 'core doctrine' does not include [ethical] teaching" (§76, cf. also §96).[3] The Report claims that ethical teaching is "woven into the fabric of Christian doctrine" (§76).

Third, a categorical distinction appears to have been drawn between core doctrine and *adiaphora*. This is the apparent logic of Motion A186, and the suggestion in the St. Michael Report Study Guide. In the latter, two non-overlapping circles are used to illustrate the difference between core doctrine and adiaphora: a larger circle representing adiaphora surrounds a smaller circle representing core doctrine.[4] The suggestion appears to be that if something does not fall within the smaller circle, then it falls in the larger circle and is therefore a matter of indifference. However, this is a false dichotomy, and once again it suggests a clear conclusion before a warranted distinction has been made. It is true that something cannot be both core doctrine and *adiaphora*, but the two options are not the only ones available to us. If a belief or practice has the property of "not being in conflict with the creeds" this does not entail that the belief or practice is necessarily *adiaphora*. In the simple two circle example, something may fall outside the larger circle, or may belong somewhere between the two lines. This is even acknowledged in the St. Michael Report: "many teachings appear to occupy a place on a scale between core doctrines and *adiaphora*" (§9). Consequently, even if the creeds exhaust the substance of core doctrine, any conclusions based on the clear distinction between it and *adiaphora* are precipitous and potentially misleading.

THE DEVELOPMENT OF DOCTRINE

The St. Michael Report discusses the development of doctrine in two ways. First, there is a consequentialist assessment. This assesses "development" in so far as it is reflected in the resulting impact on the life of the church; for example: "When true development occurs, it ultimately has healthy consequences for the life of the Church" (§13). This consequentialist assessment of what might result from changes in doctrine is a prominent concern in the Report. For example, §16 raises two questions emerging from the deliberations on the development of doctrine. The first asks whether it is theologically and doctrinally responsible to take action that may be destructive of the unity of the

Anglican Communion. The second questions whether it is theologically and doctrinally responsible to value the unity of the Communion
over what is perceived to be "an urgent gospel mandate." In a letter to
the Primates on communion, Archbishop Fred Hiltz has called these
two questions "significant questions" and they will be considered in
future dialogue.[5]

However, these questions about the potential consequences of a
change in doctrine do not speak directly to the underlying theological
questions about what a theologically and doctrinally responsible development of doctrine entails. Before assessing the impact of change, the
question whether the suggested change is theologically and doctrinally
responsible and is in fact a "gospel mandate" should be resolved.

There is also another way the development of doctrine is discussed
in the St. Michael Report, albeit only in passing. There is a description
of the development of doctrine as refinement or rearticulation. It arises
in the context of arguing against those who advocate static forms of the
expression of doctrine. Section 15 argues that sometimes the best way
to preserve revealed truth is by new and creative ways of restating it: "It
is wrong to think that there is no place for originality in the consideration of revealed truth. As new situations and human problems arise,
creativity in the rearticulation of traditional doctrine can be part of the
voice of divine wisdom." While this might be true, once again it would
require a just understanding of what constitutes traditional doctrine
before we could assess whether it had been rearticulated, or changed,
or misunderstood.

In the St. Michael Report the ambivalence between the consequentialist and rearticulation accounts of doctrinal development remains
unresolved. There is, however, a pragmatic suggestion made within the
Report: "It is commonly assumed that doctrinal certainty is required
before pastoral actions can be taken, but history also demonstrates that
clarity emerges when thought and action occur simultaneously" (§12).
For some this kind of "work in progress" model is the most important
thing said in the Report.

However, seeking "certainty" (whatever that means here) is likely not the most important outcome of a full theological reflection. And the lack of it surely does not preclude exercising judicious pastoral care. In the words of the St. Michael Report itself, the key question is whether a change in doctrine is "theologically and doctrinally responsible" (§16), a question that needs to be answered before enacting that change or acting upon that change. It is a matter of paying "full, careful, and transparent attention to the authority of [. . .] Holy Scripture and its claim upon the Church" (§23). Neglecting the difficult and cumbersome work of doctrinal reflection is not what is most expedient for the church.

It is not new in the church that many find such a call to clear and intentional theological reflection and corporate discourse onerous, if not tedious. Henry Scott Holland once wrote about a similar frustration, and his response bears repeating:

> We clamor against these intellectual complications; we cry out for the simple primitive faith. But, once again, it is a mistake of dates. We cannot ask to be as if eighteen centuries had dropped out, unnoticed,—as if the mind had slumbered since the days of Christ, and had never asked a question [. . .]. If we are asked to throw over [these] complications [. . .], we must beg those that ask to begin by throwing over the complications of this social and moral life.[6]

The only thing that has changed for us in the twenty-first century is that we have two more centuries of complications in theology and cultural diversity to consider.

HERMENEUTICS AND DOCTRINE

Since doctrine is founded on Scripture, interpreted in the context of tradition with the use of reason, biblical hermeneutics plays a role in assessing the faithfulness of a contemporary and creative expression of revealed truth. The ability to draw the line between creative expression and projection (eisegesis) is required. While some interpretations or paraphrases of Scripture might be creative, they may also by the same token fail to preserve the material meaning of the text.

The St. Michael Report at one point offers a creative paraphrase that is instructive for us to explore: "The longing for relationship [. . .] compels the person to leave the family of origin and to cleave to another, where a new community is established (Gen 2:24)" (§32). This passage in the NRSV reads: "a man leaves his father and his mother and clings to his wife, and they become one flesh." When the distinction between the complementarity of the sexes and the mutuality between persons is precisely the issue at stake in our doctrinal discussions of theological anthropology, human relationships, and sanctification, one might wish for a more consistent and accurate rendering of the biblical text than is provided by the Report's paraphrase.

Complementarity should not be confused with mutuality. Community is a real human need (§30), but finding deep personal mutuality is not the same thing as the biblical notion of the fulfillment of human complementarity. Complementarity is rooted in God's creation of men and women precisely for one another. They are equal in dignity as persons and created to become one flesh in marriage. This is the Christian foundation of the institution of marriage (§30). Moreover, this complementarity is intended to issue in personal mutuality of husband and wife, for "it is not good that the man should be alone" (Gen 2:18a, cf. §32). But, if Christian marriage is to include same-sex unions, then cogent arguments are required to establish that personal mutuality is of a higher value and separable quality from the biblical notion of biological complementarity between man and woman.

The operative assumption in the rearticulation account of doctrinal development is that faithful refinement of the revealed truth can be achieved and could be valuable. The development of doctrine is thus both continuous and discontinuous with the past, and traditional doctrinal expressions of revealed truth are open to being restated in new ways in so far as those new expressions preserve the truth more deftly. The question then becomes which expression (old or new) better captures and preserves the revealed truth. For this we need specific criteria of assessment. And to be able to address this issue we need a more refined account of the nature of doctrine and doctrinal development. Moreover, and perhaps just as importantly, we also need to resist the pessimism that says the differences between cultures make our agreement on the meaning of Scripture impossible. The Kuala Lumpur Report offers us encouragement here: "Current hermeneutical studies suggest that such pessimism is unwarranted and that the ideal of a church whose thoughts and actions are moulded by a habitual response to the message of the Bible is worth pursuing [. . .]. Knowledge of God's purposes in Scripture will always be partial in the church, yet it will be sufficient for the patient pursuit of truth and holiness" (§69).

A TYPOLOGY OF DOCTRINE

In an effort to dig the foundations deeper and to enable us to reflect more clearly and transparently on the substance of the disagreements we face, the following offers a brief outline of four views of the nature of doctrine. This presentation of these views does not aim to introduce alternate boundaries to core doctrine and *adiaphora* within a generic sense of "doctrine." Rather, it presents four competing, incompatible theories of doctrine. Each view entails a unique explanation of the nature of doctrine and doctrinal change, and only one can be correct.

The four views of doctrine considered below are: rationalist, experientialist, culturalist, and realist. In order to differentiate one from the other, four parameters are considered. Perhaps the two most prominent considerations are their *mode of expression* and *key determinants*. However, of greater import are the questions of whether these expressions, informed as they are by their determinants, are *objective* or not, and whether they are *revisable*. To be sure, this is neither an exhaustive typology nor is it sufficiently replete for the kind of full theological reflection that would be adequate to warrant doctrinal change; it is merely a place to start.

The rationalist account of doctrine takes statements of doctrine to be on par with eternal sentences—sentences that encode truth.

They are objective, context independent, and incapable of revision. This seems to be the view of doctrine argued against in §15 of the St. Michael Report when it refers to the "conservation of the old."

The experientialist theory of doctrine is at all points different from the rationalist account. For the experientialist, doctrinal statements are nondiscursive expressions of subjective experiences. As such they are inherently revisable and plastic. Instead of encoding truths, as in the rationalist account, doctrine, according to the experientialist, creates symbolic or mythical forms that express inner attitudes, feelings and sentiments. These forms are not discursive, that is, they are not statements that have substantive truth content that is open to analysis.

The culturalist model can be described as claiming that doctrinal statements reflect the socio-cultural rules of how a community uses religious language or custom. Doctrinal statements are second-order descriptions of first-order word use and practices. As cultures develop and change, so too will doctrine, as it only reflects how the community speaks and acts. The culturalist theory of doctrine rejects the experientialist reduction of doctrine to subjective, nondiscursive symbolism. The culturalist agrees with the experientialist that doctrine does not encode objective truths, but the culturalist is open to evaluating doctrine.

The realist account of doctrine is in some ways very like the culturalist theory. Statements of doctrine are not unaffected by the socio-cultural context in which they were formulated, and as such they are also revisable. They are thus neither context-free, nor encoded eternal truths. Rather they are dynamic historical expressions of eternal truth that arise within a socio-historical and cultural context. The realist differs from the culturalist in that the realist maintains that statements of doctrine are first-order statements about religious or revealed truth, and not just second-order statements about religious words and practices. Variations in modes of expression are to be expected in the realist account because of the variations in the socio-cultural and historical contexts in which doctrine is developed. However, what makes any two statements of doctrine comparable and potentially conflicting expressions is that they both try to articulate the same truths with varying perspicuity.

One further distinction between the culturalist and realist accounts of doctrine is helpful. Perhaps the greatest weakness of the culturalist theory of doctrine is that it accounts for continuity *intersubjectively and not objectively.* This means that continuity of doctrine for the culturalist hinges upon the community's intentionally self-identifying with changes in word use and practice. For the realist, however, continuity of doctrine occurs by intentionally devising and selecting verbal expressions that preserve revealed truth in more trenchant and creative ways.

At the heart of the culturalist theory is a form of constructivism. There is no objectivity of doctrinal expression other than the "objective" reporting of inter-subjective practices and language use. If a community is intentional about changing what it stipulates certain religious word use and practices should be, then in the culturalist theory those stipulations sufficiently warrant doctrinal change. What then matters most may be assessing the consequences and mitigating potential "downsides."

By contrast the realist account maintains that the central measure of continuity in doctrinal development is not an intersubjective affirmation of word use or practice, but an objective congruity of expression with what is expressed. For the realist, doctrine can be considered a "development" when it more clearly articulates the revealed truth that the doctrine was designed to express; "Development is development, and neither addition nor alteration."[7] Not only is the coherence within the community's language use and practice at issue, but the doctrine's correspondence with divine intention is to be assessed as well. This is the import and significance of asking whether a change is faithful and Spirit-led. The realist account of doctrine in effect turns culturalist constructivism on its head. The culturalist maintains that the community defines the norms of religious language use and practice, whereas the realist maintains that these define the community. Doctrine, according to the realist, has a transhistorical, transcultural and normative force that guides and directs intentional religious practice, language use and church culture. It is not only normative for the church, but is also a "normed norm." Doctrinal statements are not unrevisable, but neither are they socially constructed. In the words of Resolution 22 of Lambeth 1988,

> This Conference [. . .] affirms that God's love extends to people of every culture and that the Gospel judges every culture according to the Gospel's own criteria of truth, challenging some aspects of culture while endorsing and transforming others for the benefit of the Church and society [, and] urges the Church everywhere to work at expressing the unchanging Gospel of Christ in words, actions, names, customs, liturgies, which communicate relevantly in each contemporary society.[8]

CONCLUSION

With this brief sketch of four different theories of doctrine, the ambivalence between the consequentialist and rearticulation descriptions of doctrinal development found in the St. Michael Report can be seen as reflecting two incompatible theories of doctrine, the culturalist and the realist respectively. Both culturalist and realist accounts allow for some measure of pluralism in formal expressions of doctrine. However, only the realist account maintains the need not only for the material continuity of doctrine across cultures and history, but also for a means to assess the deftness of our transcultural and transhistorical expressions of revealed truth. The realist differs from the culturalist in that "the question of truth is primary, and its claims peremptory."[9]

Renewal of doctrine and care for God's world must be rooted in a full theological reflection if we are to be good "servants of Christ and stewards of God's mysteries" (1 Cor 4:1, NRSV). Stewardship is a salutary way of understanding our work in refining and rearticulating doctrine. It places our doctrinal reflections on a par with the aims of the writers of the creeds. Oliver Quick has stated our duty in this way: "It is the duty of the stewards of the faith in every age to make such intellectual formulations as are necessary to preserve the eternal mystery, and thus to follow the authors of the first Creeds in their essential purpose."[10] With the pressing needs of pastoral care and the Great Commission we might incline toward emphasizing pragmatic responses. With this inclination in mind, when we consider doctrine, we might ask ourselves, "How much must I give up of what religion has always been to me, that a little of the old may survive amidst the new?" Or we might ask, "How little of the old need I keep, so as not to interfere with the ready acceptance of the new?"[11] Such pragmatic approaches to doctrinal reflection are not reflective enough. And simple labels of "conservative" and "liberal," "progressive" and "traditional" simply do not do justice to the complexities of the subject.

There is much that clear and intentional theological reflection can offer, but ultimately "it is required of stewards that they be found trustworthy" (1 Cor 4:2, NRSV). The plea for deeper foundations for our theological reflections should not be taken as abstract or theoretical, because sound doctrine is never divorced from its contact with the living God:

> Let reason do its perfect work; let it heap up witness upon witness, proof upon proof. Still there will come at last the moment when the call to believe will be just the same to the complete and reasonable man as it always is to the simplest child,—the call to trust Another with a confidence which reason can justify, but can never create.[12]

Responsible theological stewardship requires clear, intentional reflection and declaration concerning both the nature of doctrine and the nature of doctrinal change. Thus it is necessary to write and appeal to the church "to contend for the faith that was once for all entrusted to the saints" (Jude 3, NRSV). For if we fail to arrive at an adequate theory of doctrine or if we operate with a tacit theory of doctrine that is incapable of preserving the revealed truth handed down to us, then we fail in our stewardship of truth and fall short of our responsibility before God.

NOTES

1. Source: http://www2.anglican.ca/primate/ptc/smr.htm (18 May 2008)

2. Source: http://www2.anglican.ca/gs2007/atsynod/minutes/june24.htm (18 May 2008)

3. Source: http://www.aco.org/ministry/theological/iatdc/docs/communion_conflict_&_hope.pdf (18 May 2008)

4. Source: http://www2.anglican.ca/about/committees/fwmc/documents/smr-studyguide.pdf, pp. 3-4 (18 May 2008)

5. Source: http://www.anglican.ca/primate/communications/2008-01-09_letter.pdf (18 May 2008)

6. Henry Scott Holland, "Faith," in *Lux Mundi* (ed. Charles Gore; 5th ed.; New York: John W. Lovell), 37-38.

7. Austin Farrer, *The Glass of Vision* (3rd ed.; Westminster: Dacre Press, 1966), 42.

8. The Secretary General of the Anglican Consultative Council 1988, *The Truth Shall Make You Free: The Lambeth Conference* 1988 (London: Church House Publishing, 1988), 219. Reaffirmed in Resolution III.14 at Lambeth 1998 (The Secretary General of the Anglican Consultative Council 1998, *The Official Report of the Lambeth Conference 1998* [Harrisburg: Morehouse Publishing, 1999], 401, cf. 197).

9. Stephen Sykes, *The Identity of Christianity* (Philadelphia: Fortress Press, 1984), 247.

10. Oliver Quick, *The Testing of Church Principles* (London: John Murray, 1919), 34.

11. Aubrey Moore, "The Christian Doctrine of God," in *Lux Mundi*, 47.

12. Henry Scott Holland, "Faith," in *Lux Mundi*, 43.

SECTION TWO

On the Holy Spirit

CHAPTER FOUR

Does the Holy Spirit Teach New Truths?

Ephraim Radner

What does the Holy Spirit do? If we could be sure of this, perhaps we could also be capable of judging rightly the things of this world and our relationship to them as creatures of God and children of God's truth. The question, however, is too broad to address comprehensively. But in the context of a church's attempt to discern the truth about a course of action viewed by many as wrong and certainly as previously untried—same-sex blessings, in this case—we might limit our question to whether the Holy Spirit does "new" things, or provides "new revelations" or even leads into "new truths." The question of the "new," while hardly exhausting the work of the Holy Spirit, can perhaps offer us a means of framing such a larger pneumatology in a practical way.

In the modern era, Christians have been increasingly averse to seeking continuities within the dispensations of God's historical purposes. The notion that Christ's own work might be continuous with God's consistent work in time has, often unconsciously, been seen as providing the gospel's detractors a tool with which to diminish the evangelical particularity of their faith. To claim that "Christianity is as old as Creation," to use the phrase popularized by Matthew Tindal's 1730 book of that title, was to open the door to Deism, "natural" religion, and finally atheism. The modern "evangelical" (taking the word generally) will wish, therefore, to stress the "new" of the "New Testament," and the discontinuity between this "new" and what is "old." In this way, the modern Christian apologist is often more comfortable with the old Marcionites than with new "scientific" uniformitarianism.

But, however apologetically understandable, is this response in fact true to the Christian gospel itself? For within Scripture, creation is something *established*, not something refashioned dispensationally. Within the scriptural order of creation, life is given and taken away, or renewed and redirected, as the psalms (e.g. Ps 104) among other books make clear. But the order of creation *itself* is not constantly refashioned. Whatever the world is, it is not invented anew "in Christ" in a way that goes beyond the order of God's initial grace in creating at all. This is the burden of the "six days" and the "Sabbath rest," that is, that creation is given and enjoyed and rested in, and not only in humanly perceived, but in a divinely established manner (Gen 2:2; Exod 20:8-11). Even an "evangelical" like Karl Barth has insisted upon this.

Does God then do nothing "new"? What of the "new things" promised in Isaiah? Yet if we look at a key "declaration" like Isaiah 42:9—"See, the former things have come to pass, and new things I now declare . . ."—we see that the context of this promise of "new things" within the prophet's words points to the Creator (42:5) who *restores* Israel to the purpose from which it has fallen. What is "new" is that Israel shall now be reformed and equipped to be a "light" to the nations through her obedience and devotion to God (cf. vv. 17ff.), where the law is now finally and properly "magnified" (21). What is "new" is the possibility to fulfill what is "old."

Again, when Isaiah proclaims God's giving of a "new" heaven and earth (65:17), he speaks not of a removal of creation for something different to replace it, but of the miracle of survival and faithfulness and finally usefulness, and of a remnant taken out from a punished and destroyed Israel. Mercy and forgiveness, and the sheer survival of the remnant is analogized to birth itself, that is, to creation out of death. It is not a replacement theory that Isaiah proposes here, but a resurrection theory, as it were, presenting the grace of God that brings life out of the crucible of divine wrath.

Thus, it is *in* the divine given-ness of creation—itself sheer grace—that "newness" arises. And it is in the given-ness of the law that a "new" covenant is given, new not in its content, but in its means of receipt and execution. Hence the covenant (Jer 31:31) of the heart and spirit (Ezek 36:26) is a renewal of obedience to the established covenant of God (Ezek 36:27). It stands as God's performance of Israel's actual duty of obedience, which she herself cannot attain (Ezek 18:31). "Newness" pertains to the merciful efficacy of the divine assumption of the burdens of obedience.

The divine assumption of obedience is clearly that aspect of the promise that is "fulfilled" in the self-proclamation of Jesus. It informs, for instance, the general sense of the character of "newness" in the "new testament" itself: what is "new" here is the "covenant of blood" given in Jesus' own flesh and self-offering, an offering in which the disobedience of the world is undone by his obedience. The Last Supper is the most obvious statement of this (Mark 14:24 etc., and 1 Cor 11:25, but also Heb 8:13, 18; 9:15; 10:20), but it is important to see how this particularized action is continuous with the prophecies of newness in Isaiah.

Similarly, where Paul speaks of "new creation," it is in reference to the "renewal" of creation's purpose through the assumption of its order and the pain of this order by God himself in the flesh of Jesus. Joined to *this*, the Christian is him- or herself "renewed" in the obedience of the flesh to the created and creative purposes of God. The famous verse in 2 Cor 5:17 must be read in the context of at least vv. 14–21, where Christ's death "for all" (17), by "becoming sin for us" (21), might transform us into the "righteousness of God," not in a new form, but newly full and rightly ordered. The language of "reconciliation" is bound up with this. *Katalagge* is commercial language of agreed-upon exchange, now transposed to personal relationships. "Reconciliation" in this context represents the re-ordering and re-establishment thereby of a *covenant*. The "testament" or "covenant" is "new" because it is "renewed" through the readjustment of the burden of its demands, in this case, through the assumption of those burdens by God himself. (Hence, the same word for "reconciliation" is used by Paul in 1 Cor 7:11, regarding the maintenance of the marriage relationship between husband and wife; it stands in contrast to divorce and remarriage.)

The discussion, finally, of the Spirit in 2 Corinthians 3 takes place within this set of understandings: Paul links the new covenant of Jeremiah and Ezekiel explicitly with the Spirit (vv. 3 and 6), and the purpose of this covenant is thus seen as granted to the Christian pneumatically. But how shall we understand this new "spiritual" covenant? It is built upon God's creative will, ordered towards his longstanding purpose, and emerges out of judgment and suffering. Second Corinthians 4:5 is the key here: the act of preaching Christ Jesus is the place where the renewal of the covenant takes place in the lives of men and women, and is given its lived form. Thus, faithfulness to this testament is given in Paul's own life through his service of obedience and suffering on behalf of the Corinthians (4:7 ff., and, as a kind of bracketing *inclusio*, 6:4–10).

The notion of a "new commandment," of which Jesus speaks in John (13:24) and that is taken up by John himself again later (1 John 2:8), finds its explication here. In the first place, what is "new" about the commandment is that it is bound to the renewal of the covenant itself, but precisely in the form by which God had long ago described it, viz. through the assumption of the covenant's burdens by God himself for the sake of restoring Israel's life through forgiveness. This is the "love" which Jesus not only "commands," but of course more properly embodies, through the fact that he *is* God's own assumption of the covenant's human burdens: *this is love* (1 John 4:10).

Hence, in the second place, "loving one another" becomes the "preaching of the Gospel of Christ Jesus" for the sake of "obedience" (cf. Rom 1:5, 15:18, 16:26; 1 Pet 1:2) and Paul's own embodiment of this preaching is itself the "image" of Christ. In this way, the "new" commandment is also "old," and from the beginning (1 John 2:7), because it is God's own covenanting self that consistently restores his relationship with Israel and finally the world for the sake of fulfilling a single purpose. And Paul's way of preaching the gospel—that is, fulfilling the old/new commandment that is God's own will "from the beginning"—is then commended to the church at large: the "new self" (or "new man") of Eph 4:24 and Col 3:10 is a being created for holiness and righteousness, "good works" (Eph 2:10), but given now in the great restoration of covenant that is the cross of Christ (cf. Eph 2:15), the blood of the new covenant. The fact that this "new man," after the image of Christ and the Creator both, represents not a new set of rules, but the "old" way of life given by God in creation, is made clear by the long discussion in e.g. Eph 4:25–5:21 or Col 3:1–4:6 that describes quite concretely what "newness" constitutes: exhortations against lying, thievery, anger, idolatry, malice, covetousness, fornication, and drunkenness, and in favor of honesty, purity, hard work, forgiveness and gentleness. None of this is "new" in any way, and indeed is bound to the words of the Scriptures in their particularity and coherence. Indeed, they represent the unchanging and very image of God (Eph 5:1). Similarly, the stark contrast by Paul in Rom 7:6 between the "newness of the Spirit" and the "oldness of the letter" represents, in the first instance, not a matter of new vs. old "content," but of new vs. old *powers* or efficacies for "fruit" (7:4), given by participation and membership in the "body" of Christ, the "fulfiller" of the law (Rom 10:4).

How then shall we describe the work of the Holy Spirit with respect to "newness"? However we decide to do this, our description must remain coherent with the "newness" that is Jesus' own covenantal restoration. And in fact, key discussions of the Holy Spirit's work underline this coherence. Take, for instance, the words of Jesus in John 16:7–14 (ESV):

> Nevertheless, I tell you the truth: it is to your advantage that I go
> away, for if I do not go away, the Helper will not come to you. But if
> I go, I will send him to you. And when he comes, he will convict the

world concerning sin and righteousness and judgment: concerning
sin, because they do not believe in me; concerning righteousness,
because I go to the Father, and you will see me no longer; concerning judgment, because the ruler of this world is judged. I still have
many things to say to you, but you cannot bear them now. When
the Spirit of truth comes, he will guide you into all the truth, for he
will not speak on his own authority, but whatever he hears he will
speak, and he will declare to you the things that are to come. He
will glorify me, for he will take what is mine and declare it to you.

It is verse 13 here, which speaks of the Spirit's "guiding into all truth,"
that has proved the most interesting place of focus in current discussion. Yet this verse cannot be read or understood apart from the work
Jesus describes as the content of this truth (never identified, it should
be noted, as a "new truth"), that is, verses 8–11. This is what the Spirit
"will do," and it logically founds the shape of the "truth" into which the
disciples will be "guided." And what is this work? It is the work of "conviction" (v. 8), a word that is generally used in terms of face-to-face presentation of an otherwise ignored, denied, or avoided reality. (In Matt
18:15, it is used when one Christian confronts another with a matter
of mutual concern over sin and harm.) In this case, the Spirit's work
constitutes the exposure of divine reconciliation, as even Paul describes
it, in terms of suffering judgment. The world the Spirit "convicts" is all
of humanity, as Israel extends (or rejects) her life and her missionary
calling within it; the "going away" of Jesus through which the Spirit
accomplishes this convicting exposure refers to Jesus' own resurrection and ascension which is, in fact, the completion of the incarnation,
as John presents it; the judgment of the world's ruler out of which the
Spirit's conviction emerges is none other than the cross itself to which
Jesus earlier refers in John 12:31. All together, this work of the Spirit
coincides with the "new testament" of blood in which "God so loved the
world that he sent his Son" (John 3:16).

The Spirit's work is given *in this*, but also, and as its flip side, it is
given in the way that this work "preaches the gospel," that is, preaches
the truth of God's work for the sake of the "new man" of obedience.

That the disciples cannot yet "bear" this work at the time of Jesus' teaching (John 16:12), is a mark of the work itself, that is, of the cross (the "bearing" here pointing to the cross that is "borne" by Jesus in John 19:17). But once "borne" in Christ, once joined in his death, what the Spirit will say is precisely congruent with the "revealed" character of Isa 42:9 and 48:6: the purpose of God from the foundation of the world, bound up in creation itself. It is not possible to pry apart the truths of the Spirit from the covenant given by the Spirit (2 Cor 3), a covenant bound up with the work of God in Christ in assuming the "old" covenant's burdens, and hence effecting "reconciliation." "Truth," that is, is consistent with the purposes of God given in creation and furthered by the covenants; and the Holy Spirit's service to the truth is not to *another* truth but to just *this* one.

That is why John 16:12–15 refers to the Father's purposes, which the Son has taken for himself: "He will glorify me, for he will take what is mine and declare it to you. All that the Father has is mine; therefore I said that he will take what is mine and declare it to you." This suggests that the Holy Spirit's work is indeed the explicating of the Scripture— that is, the Old Testament—for the sake of bringing into light the coherence of the Scriptures as created covenant. "We declare unto you that which was from the beginning" (1 John 1:1, 3).

When Jesus himself speaks, therefore, of that which is "from the beginning"—in Matthew, for instance, he says this with regard to the creation of male and female and the nature of their unitive vocation (Matt 9:4 and 8)—he is speaking of a particularly "pneumatic" reality, a reality quite literally of the Holy Spirit. Just as "from the beginning" we have heard of him and seen him and even touched him (1 John 1:1), and he himself is "in the beginning" (John 1:1), and assumes his task from the Father's love, even the covenantal task of the whole creation, "from the foundation of the world" (John 17:24; Eph 1:4; 1 Pet 1:20; Rev 13:8; cf. Matt 13:35), *even so* "from the beginning" he is bound up, and the Spirit is also so bound, with the creation of male and female in this way. Indeed, the term translated as "foundation" in all these cases is a sexually-charged word—the sowing of seed and sperm—indicating God's life-giving as well as material "building up." This particular "foundation" marks the fact that the purposes of creation, in its life-bearing aspects, are those caught up in the very reality of Christ, so that what is the Father's in creating male and female, for instance, is also the Son's, is "mine," and the Holy Spirit's work is to make this "mine" of Jesus bear the burden of what is "my Father's" "from the beginning." What is "new"—the fruitfulness of the Spirit's drawing us into the life of Jesus' death and resurrection—is necessarily "old," for it is given in the same act as the creation of male and female. So Paul himself argues in Eph 5:22–33.

More broadly, Jesus explains the imperative given to those who would understand this relationship in terms of teaching, particularly teaching for the sake of the kingdom of God, in these terms. In Matt 13:51f., for instance, he speaks of the disciples (and hence of the church) as "scribes of the kingdom": " 'Have you understood all these things?' They said to him, 'Yes.' And he said to them, 'Therefore every scribe who has been trained for the kingdom of heaven is like a master of a house, who brings out of his treasure what is new and what is old.'" The issue here is not, as one line of traditional interpretation of these verses has put it, a pastoral need to wean the Jews or other converts only gradually from their "old ways," and hence Jesus is warning his disciples to move slowly in the face of his "new" message. Rather, Jesus is describing how the fruits of God's creative purposes, fulfilled in the kingdom, are continuous with the history of his revelation, to which the scribe gives thoughtful notice. True love, the Spirit's life itself, seeks out this continuity; so it is that Jesus himself, in his phraseology, is drawing on Song of Songs 7:13, where the ardor of affection brings the gift of fruits "new" and "old."

In this light we can better understand the pneumatic dynamics at work in the famous (and some might think now notorious) decision regarding the parameters of gentile "inclusion" described in Acts 15. It simply is not proper to see the decision here by the young church as the apprehension of a new revelation of a new truth, such that what seems "good to the Holy Spirit" (15:28) is the embrace of such a new truth.

For those who have, more recently, made this argument (especially as a warrant for claiming a similar "new truth" taught by the Spirit in relation to same-sex relations), the "leading of the Spirit," now parsing John 16:13, is precisely a leading into the *newness* of Jesus' truth, a truth heretofore unknown. But this argument is based on an erroneous understanding both of the actual character of the decision made by the apostles, and of the Spirit's relation to "newness." Rather, as more recent study of the text's recounting of this episode makes clear, what is at stake in this event is the recognition that the gentile inclusion is indeed *continuous* with the creative will of God "*from the beginning*" (15:18), and that this is rightly attested to by the Scriptures themselves which "agree" on the matter (15:15).

"Agreement" here is the quite practical notion of saying the "same thing," and is transliterated as "symphonic," something that the strong and adversarial contrast of "old" and "new" cannot permit. The adversarial or at best dispensational way of putting the contrast, instead of interpreting "old" and "new" as we have done in terms of God's single covenantal purpose for creation, narrowly applies to pneumatic discernment the dynamics of something like Luke 5:36, where it appears as if the "old" and the "new" are incompatible. (In this saying, Jesus discusses the difficulty of joining together old and new patches and garments. But the saying is better understood in terms of the disciple's *response* to the truth, than as a description of the nature of Jesus' truth itself. That is, God's truth may be offered by Jesus in new ways, and must surely be apprehended appropriately to these ways; but the truth, like God's Word, "endures forever" [Isa 40:8; 1 Pet 1:25.]) It is in this "agreement" or "symphony" of the Scriptures that the parameters of the gentile inclusion agreed to by the apostles is seen not as in fact something novel, but as the application of the "old" law of either (in this interpreters today give alternative, but hardly contradictory explication) Noachide order (rabbinic regulations for gentiles based on an elaboration of Gen 9:1–18) or the Levitical specification of the same (in e.g. Lev 18 and 19), as applied more explicitly to sojourners within Israel. What is "new" in the decision described in Acts 15, if one wishes to use such a term here, is the *efficacious apprehension* itself in this place and time of something long-standing within the order of creation, as already exposed within the Scriptures.

Thus, the Holy Spirit's operative mission has consistently been viewed by the church as the interpreter of the *given*, the Scriptures of God and their symphonic word regarding the incarnation of the Word, through which the true character of creation's purpose as ordered by God is properly and rootedly explicated. When the third-century Montanists, as argued in Tertullian, sought to press this interpretive role of the Spirit into an area that evidently and finally, by their own admission, moved *outside* the actual form and content of the Scriptures—outside their plain "agreement" and explicit coherence—the Montanists themselves recognized that they had moved beyond and outside this larger church (they were willing to take the name of "Spirituals," over and against those other "natural" men), just as Catholics from their perspective saw the same. So Tertullian writes, in a key text regarding the rejected Montanist reach into pneumatic innovation:

> But the Paraclete, having many things to teach fully which the Lord
> deferred till He came, (according to the pre-definition), will begin
> by bearing emphatic witness to Christ, (as being) such as we believe
> (Him to be), together with the whole order of God the Creator,
> and will glorify Him, and will "bring to remembrance" concern-
> ing Him. And when He has thus been recognised (as the promised
> Comforter), on the ground of the cardinal rule, He will reveal those
> "many things" which appertain to disciplines; while the integrity of
> His preaching commands credit for these (revelations), albeit they
> be "novel," inasmuch as they are now in course of revelation, albeit
> they be "burdensome," inasmuch as not even now are they found
> bearable: (revelations), however, of none other Christ than (the
> One) who said that He had withal "other many things" which were
> to be fully taught by the Paraclete, no less burdensome to men of
> our own day than to them, by whom they were then "not yet able to
> be borne."
>
> *On Monogamy* 2 (*ANF* 4:60)[1]

We should be aware that Tertullian's worry was over the Christian's strength to resist persecution nobly, and hence a new strength of self-denial was demanded for the burden of the times. Yet, despite the fact that Tertullian saw this reach beyond the letter as justified in part because of its press into greater *rigour* of discipline—the Spirit could hardly speak "new" truths on matters that involved a *permissive* revelation!—the rest of the church understood this claim to pneumatic innovation as unacceptable precisely because it sought to go beyond the coherence of scriptural, and thereby divinely created, purpose.

Does the Spirit speak or teach "new truths"? The answer must be that given by those as diverse as Saint-Cyran, Frederick Douglass, and Mary McCarthy: there is no "new truth." There is rather the truth of the one God, upon which creation is founded, to which the Scriptures are ordered, for which Jesus Christ has died and risen again, and within which the Spirit gives evidence through the calling and equipping of a Church to follow in his way. Would that we might be newly cognizant of this fact.

NOTES

1. Tertullian, *On Monogamy,* in *The Anti-Nicene Fathers* (ed. Alexander Roberts and James Donaldson; 1885-1887; 10 vols.; repr.; Peabody, Mass: Hendrickson, 1994).

CHAPTER FIVE

"Spirit-led":

John 16:12–13 and "Core doctrine" in Christian Antiquity

Robert D. Sider

The St. Michael Report has thrust the expression "core doctrine" into the forefront of current debates in the Anglican Church of Canada. The definition given to the phrase, "in the sense of being creedal" (which is further explicated as "the common affirmation of the three Creeds")—carries important consequences. Chiefly, it calls us back to the world of Christian antiquity in which the creeds originated, imposing upon us an obligation to become familiar with that world, to understand it, and to "converse" with it in order both to measure and enrich our experience by sharing theirs, and to recognize the cultural boundaries within which the creeds were formulated. In doing so we shall admit that in our debates "core doctrine" offers no refuge from the "cultural relativity" of Scripture.

It is not my intention here, however, to force such a conclusion. The first step is to converse with our predecessors, to respond to their narratives with our own concerns, to check our thinking against theirs—this has been, and is, one supposes, the *via anglicana*, the Anglican Way. It is, perhaps, characteristic of our thinking that we should, in our present hesitations, seek to know whether synodal actions are "Spirit-led." "Spirit-led" is an image stamped with the imprimatur of Scripture, and an image that finds its closest relevance, I would argue, to our present distresses in John 16:12–13. I should like, therefore, to hear the voice of the Fathers as they bring these verses to bear on their own situation, and to respond to their formulations with a voice from ours.

Given the limitations of space, I choose three writers representing three different centuries, and, as it happens, all from cities on the northern coast of Africa, where Christianity flourished until the Arab invasions imposed Islam: Tertullian (fl. 190–220) from Carthage, Didymus the Blind (313–398) from Alexandria, and Augustine (354–430), bishop of Hippo Regius. It is worth recalling the pleasant irony that while all these were vigorous defenders of orthodoxy, only Augustine escaped the charge of heresy! The translations that follow are mine.

TERTULLIAN

Tertullian breaks upon the Christian scene like a flash of lightning in a cloudless sky. We know nothing certain of his background. Apparently a convert from paganism, he emerges to view in 197 as an outspoken apologist for Christianity. Within a decade he had moved from emerging Catholic Christianity to the professedly Spirit-led, indeed, Spirit-propelled, brand of Montanism known in Carthage. Within another decade he disappears from sight, except for an untrustworthy recollection by Jerome, and for his thunderous writings that offer the first known formulations in Latin of what would become Trinitarian and Christological orthodoxy. His treatise *De monogamia—On Single Marriage* belongs to his later Montanist period, and is remarkable for its appeal to the "Rule of Faith"—something very nearly like our "core doctrine." As a Montanist Tertullian distinguishes here between the *psychici*, "carnal Christians" and the *spiritales*, "spiritual Christians": he derogatorily characterizes as "carnal" the traditionalist Catholics who maintain the church's view that a Christian whose spouse has died may legitimately remarry; his own revisionist view looks for a higher moral order in the community of the Spirit, for whose members, the "spiritual" Christians, living as they do in the sphere of the Spirit, one marriage only is sufficient.

De monogamia 2.1–4 (*Corpus Christianorum Series Latina* 2 1229–30):

> And so the carnal Christians bring reproach upon the discipline of monogamy by calling it a heresy. In fact, they are compelled to deny the Paraclete primarily because they suppose he has instituted a novel discipline, and, indeed, one that is altogether too harsh. Hence we must first of all determine in a general discussion whether our view assumes that the Paraclete has taught anything at all that can be reckoned either as new, as opposed to Catholic tradition, or burdensome, as opposed to that "light burden" of the Lord. Now on both counts the Lord himself has given a verdict in these words: "I still have many things to say to you, but you are not able to bear them; when the holy Spirit has come, he [*ille*] will lead you into all the truth" [John 16:12–13]. Here he [Christ] has quite clearly indicated that the Spirit will teach what can be considered as both new (as never published) and sometimes burdensome (as unpublished for that reason.)
>
> Therefore, you say, "On the basis of this type of argument anything at all that is new and onerous can be ascribed to the Paraclete, even if it comes from an adversary spirit." By no means! A spirit would be revealed as adversary from the different character of its preaching, first falsifying the "Rule of Faith" and so distorting the pattern of discipline.
>
> . . . One must first be unorthodox in relation to the doctrine of God, then one becomes unorthodox in relation to the ordinances of God. The Paraclete himself, having many things to teach, will first affirm the sort of Christ in which we believe, along with the entire order of our creator God: him he will glorify; of him he will speak. Then, recognized from that principle "Rule" [i.e., "core doctrine"], he will reveal the many other things that belong to discipline, while

the unblemished orthodoxy of his preaching elicits our confidence
in those "other things"—granted they are new, inasmuch as they are
only now revealed, granted, too, that they are burdensome since not
even now are they being borne . . .

Set within the context of our current debates, this passage may seem
somewhat disconcerting. We recognize here an appeal to the "leading
of the Spirit" that will take us beyond, or outside, the prescriptions of
Scripture and the catholic tradition; in this respect the parallel with
our own situation in the Anglican Church of Canada is clear. On the
other hand, the argument is made to validate a disciplinary direction
that goes quite counter to that into which we are pressed: Tertullian
would see the leading of the Spirit in the tightening of discipline, we
want to know if the Spirit will lead us to relax the traditional discipline, to "widen the circle," so to speak. Nevertheless, the passage
has implications deserving our attention. In the first place, we can
catch the tenor of debate among those Carthaginian Christians of the
early third century: "You wish to innovate in discipline; how will you
justify it? You claim the leading of the Spirit; give us the proof that the
innovation is Spirit-led." Secondly, Tertullian's appeal to the "Rule of
Faith" is hauntingly like our own appeal to "core doctrine." There is,
however, a striking qualification: for Tertullian it is not enough simply
to affirm the Christ; we must affirm the *sort of* [Latin *qualis*] Christ the
Catholic tradition affirms. Most Anglicans can affirm the creeds; fewer
would affirm all the articles of the creeds in the sense the Catholic
tradition has understood them. The dissolution of the traditional sense
of the articles of the creeds renders "core doctrine" as a touchstone
of orthodox integrity meaningless. Finally, we should observe as an
historical fact –and with gratitude—that in the matter of monogamy
the wisdom of Catholic consensus in support of Catholic tradition
prevailed over the perceived leading of the Spirit.

DIDYMUS THE BLIND

Didymus lived in a century which, through exile, excommunication, death and innumerable anathemas, established the Nicene Creed as the litmus test of Trinitarian orthodoxy. Though Didymus was a Greek speaker, his work *De spiritu sancto* (*On the Holy Spirit*) has survived only in the Latin translation of Jerome. Clearly a response to the burning issue of his day, the *De spiritu sancto* comes to us as an exploration of the relation of the "persons" of the Trinity. The sixteenth chapter of the Gospel of St. John, and its verses twelve and thirteen would serve this purpose well. But Didymus' suggestive exposition is not without implications for us.

De spiritu sancto 31, 34 (*Patrologia Graeca* 39 [electronic version] 1061B-D, 1063C-1064A)

> That Holy Spirit who comes in the name of the Son of God, sent by the Father, will teach all things to those who have been perfected in faith—all, that is to say, that is spiritual and intellectual, in a word, all the sacraments of word and wisdom. Moreover, he will teach not as a teacher and instructor of a discipline that is acquired from some outside source . . . but he insinuates into the mind the knowledge of divine things. For thus the Father also teaches his disciples . . . Likewise the Son of God and the wisdom of God and the truth teach . . . not by skill but by nature. These same teachings given by the Father and the Son to the hearts of believers the Holy Spirit ministers to those who have ceased to be carnal, for "the carnal person [biblical Greek *psychicos*, Jerome's Latin *animalis*] does not receive the things of the Spirit" [1 Cor 2:14], judging that the things said [by the Spirit] are folly. Those, however, who have purged their minds will be filled with the instructions of the Holy Spirit, that is, with the words of wisdom and knowledge, and can say, "God has revealed to us through the Holy Spirit" [1 Cor 2:10]. God bestows upon those who have thus prepared themselves the spirit of wisdom and of revelation for the knowledge of himself. Those who receive the spirit of wisdom and revelation from no other source than the Holy Spirit become wise, and by the Spirit understand the Lord and whatever is of God's will.

[Didymus now refers the sentence "He will lead you into all the truth" specifically to the disciples who, at the time Jesus spoke were still not "spiritual," but would have become spiritual when they passed from the dead letter of the Law to the vivifying Spirit. He then continues:]

> In what follows [John 16:12–13] about the Spirit of truth who is sent by the Father, and is the Paraclete, the Saviour says: "He will not speak of himself," that is, not without me and without my will and the will of the Father, since my will and the will of the Father are inseparable . . . In the Trinity speaking and talking do not follow our human pattern of conversation, but the pattern appropriate to incorporeal natures, especially that of the Trinity, which implants its will into the hearts of believers and of those worthy to hear it.

Two points arrest us in our reading. First, Didymus describes a context—a sort of school—in which the teaching of the Holy Spirit (and hence the leading of the Holy Spirit) must occur. But if the language of learning is appropriately pedagogical, the mode of learning transcends scholarly expectations: it is not the bright mind but the pure heart that the Spirit instructs; it is not the language of debate but the silent insinuation of the divine will by which the Spirit leads. Second, Trinitarian orthodoxy here is not for Didymus a scholastic test of legitimacy. The Trinity is, rather, a dynamic relationship into which we, as believers, are conveyed, and it is when we hold fast in that relationship with the Three Persons that the Spirit inspires and leads us into truth. To legitimize our truth by declaring that it does not conflict with the doctrine of the Trinity is barren scholasticism, if not Jesuitical casuistry. Rather, with Didymus, we must find in the Trinity the creative centre of our Christian experience, from which then all change and progress may proceed.

AUGUSTINE

Augustine's immense series of *Tractates* [sermons] *on the Gospel of John* are the work of an experienced bishop, and one can see reflected in these sermons the concerns of a bishop who brought to the episcopacy the recollections of a multi-faceted life: a mother's faith abandoned due to the "problems" of Scripture; a dissolute life in youth; conversion to the Manichaean heresy; a distinguished career as a teacher and orator, in due time a conversion back to his mother's faith, a contest with the schismatic and disruptive Donatists of North Africa in which the Catholics had been less than evenly matched. Thus in the short passage that follows below, it is characteristic of him to observe carefully the variant in the biblical text, to address almost instinctively the epistemological question of the certainty and extent of Christian knowledge, and to decry the subtle appeal to the role of the Spirit on the part of those whose dissolute lives demonstrate their heretical mentality.

In evangelium Johannis Tractatus 96.4–5 (*Corpus Christianorum Series Latina* 36 571–2)

> Therefore, most beloved, make progress in charity, which is shed abroad in your hearts by the Holy Spirit. He will teach you all the truth, or, as we find in other codices, "He will lead you in all truth." . . . Thus it will not be from exterior teachers that you will learn what the Lord at that time did not wish to say, but we will all be "taught by God" [John 6:45]. In this way, what you have learned and believed about God through readings and discourses offered by others ["the exterior teachers"] . . . you will be able to grasp by the mind itself ["the interior teacher"]. But if that interior teacher . . . wished to speak to us inwardly about the incorporeal nature of God in the same way he speaks to the holy angels, who always look upon the face of the Father—such words we would not be able to bear. Accordingly, that statement of his, "[the Spirit] will teach you all truth," or "will lead you into all the truth" cannot, I think, be fulfilled in this life in the mind of anyone, for who, as long as he lives in this body that is undergoing corruption and weighs down the soul, can possibly know all the truth? . . .
>
> And so, most beloved, I admonish you in the charity of Christ to beware of those seductive and filthy followers of shameless obscenities, of whom the Apostle said, "It is a disgrace even to speak of the things they do in secret" [Eph 5:12]. Avoid them, lest when they begin to teach their frightful obscenities, which no human ears can bear, they say that these are the very things of which the

Lord said, "I have many things to tell you, but you are not able to bear them now," and they affirm that it is through the Holy Spirit that they can bear these unclean and forbidden things. There are evils that no human sense of shame can bear, and there are good things that the limitations of the human mind cannot bear . . . "Be renewed, therefore, in the spirit of your mind [Eph 4:23], and understand what is the will of God . . . [Rom 12:2], so that rooted and grounded in charity, you might be able to understand with all the saints what is the length, height, breadth and depth; to know as well the surpassing love of the knowledge of Christ [sic], that you might be filled with all the fullness of God" [Eph 3:17–19]. In this way the Holy Spirit will teach you all the truth when, more and more he will shed charity abroad in your hearts.

When Augustine speaks here of the "interior teacher," we recall that most unique of his early dialogues, *On the Teacher*, where, in conversation with his son Adeodatus, he concludes that genuine knowledge of universals is possible only because we all have an inner light, who is Christ [*De magistro* 11.38]. Here in the *Tractates* that inner light, that inner teacher, has become the Holy Spirit, shed abroad in our hearts, who will lead us into all truth. And then, characteristically, Augustine draws back: not quite!—as long as we live in this body we cannot possibly know all the truth; not even the Spirit can nullify the epistemological consequences of the physical reality of our human nature. A sober warning: honest Christians must always meet with humbling scepticism their claim to be Spirit-led.

But Augustine is willing to make judgments. Not all Christians are honest Christians; some who bear the name of Christ are seducers, appealing to the Spirit as the proof of their integrity. Of these we must beware. We could wish that Augustine had at this point said more: what were these "obscenities?" why does he call them obscenities? is it through our "interior teacher" that we recognize what is and should be truly forbidden? does the Christian community itself as a corporate body have an "interior teacher"? How is the voice of our "teacher" known? It is a list of desiderata that leads us back to scepticism.

On the one hand, then, our reading of these three ancient Christian writers on John 16:12–13 leads to a sort of hermeneutic of scepticism, for these passages point to the difficulty inherent in the question General Synod has asked of its Theological Commission: trustworthy knowledge of the leading of the Spirit is simply not ours to have. On the other hand, our distant predecessors point us in directions that promise to be fruitful in our present circumstances, inviting us to find in catholic consensus a reasonable assurance that our synodal actions will be forward-looking precisely as they are rooted in a vital tradition of an enduring Christian faith, and to find in the creeds not only documents that attest orthodoxy or legitimize majority votes, but living doctrine that becomes for us a theological matrix out of which can emerge an expansive corporate experience of the divine in the power of which we move forward.

CHAPTER SIX

When the Spirit Leads

Ronald A. N. Kydd

Visiting one of the parishes in the Diocese of Toronto recently, I sat listening appreciatively to the homily being delivered by the incumbent. One question she asked particularily caught my attention—"Are we open to the Spirit?" She had been talking about things happening in the parish, and she was looking into the future. It was clear that she thought being open to the Spirit was a good idea.

After many years of active ministry in a Pentecostal denomination before becoming an Anglican, I was accustomed to that kind of language, but more of that later. Here was an Anglican priest talking like a Pentecostal. In fact, I have been hearing references to the leading of the Spirit as well as openness to the Spirit fairly often since I joined the Anglican church. Usually those using these phrases did so in the context of discussions of human sexuality, and usually they were implying that there should be some change in the way in which the Anglican church responds to the homosexual community. A prime example of this is a recent publication by a homosexual special-interest group from the United States. In what is a strategy paper for their "Canterbury Campaign" drafted in preparation for the upcoming Lambeth

Conference, they express the hope that bishops will "hear what the Spirit is saying to the church" and embrace their position.[1]

But that is not the only context in which I have encountered this kind of language being used in contemporary discourse. I have come across the "leading of the Spirit" associated with stereotype-breaking diversity in employment patterns, social concerns, religious involvement, and political alignment among American Latinos,[2] with Roman Catholic development of an approach to world missions[3] and with Anselm, Archbishop of Canterbury's articulation of his theology.[4] Occasionally, I have wondered what "s/Spirit" people were taking about, but I have decided that it has not been anything so esoteric as the Hegelian World Spirit (*Geist*) unfolding its nature through universal history. Usually reference to Christianity has been somewhere nearby in the discussion, leading me to believe that I could assume, perhaps naively, some connection with the church's historical understanding of the Holy Spirit.

As I implied earlier, language about the "moving of the Spirit" has been common among revivalist movements in the Church. Martin Luther faced it from some of the "enthusiasts" he had to deal with, and it certainly characterizes those in Pentecostal and charismatic circles, who, of course, account for a rapidly growing segment of global Christianity. Philip Jenkins has said that by 2050 Pentecostals will equal the number of Hindus in the world and double the number of Buddhists.[5] In addition to that a 1994 study showed that 12 million of the 55 million Roman Catholics in the United States saw themselves as "charismatics or Pentecostalists."[6] It is a bit of a surprise to find self-styled "progressivists" resorting to talking about the Spirit now, and one wonders why.

It is safe to say that this kind of "Spirit language" is comparatively new among the older denominations, at least in the western world. Emeritus professor at McGill, Douglas Hall, not a known conservative, in 1999 talked about a different language shift which took place about a century ago among the same denominations. Then, he said, it was done in an attempt to make themselves as attractive as possible to an increasingly uninterested and jaded society. This "progressive religion" (his term) cancelled out words like sin, the demonic, and spiritual death because it feared that they would not be culturally acceptable. The result? They were left without a vocabulary to assess the horrors of World War I. And further, ". . . it reconciled God and man by deifying the latter and humanizing the former," all in an attempt to maintain its place in society.[7] As the twentieth century unrolled, declining numbers showed that the attempt had been in vain.

In the light of all of this, spending some time attempting to bring the idea of being "led by the Spirit" into focus seems important. The idea I want to develop is as follows: the directive activity of the Holy Spirit finds its essential orientation in Christ Jesus. I will take two steps. First, I will look at the idea itself, and, second, I will reflect on how it relates to our Lord, Jesus Christ.

BEING LED BY THE SPIRIT

Historic Christianity has taught that salvation is offered to humanity through the Christ event. With the sacraments playing their roles, the human person is drawn into a life-giving relationship with God through faith in Christ. In the encyclical *Redemptoris Missio,* Pope John Paul II talked about a conversion, meaning ". . . accepting, by a personal decision, the saving sovereignty of Christ and becoming his disciple." Jesus Christ is the son of whom John 3:16 speaks.

However, acknowledging that the avenue to God has been opened by Christ, theologians then have struggled to find ways to talk about the process by which individuals experience salvation. The "application" of what God has done in Christ appears to be the unique theatre of activity for the Holy Spirit. It has been suggested that the extraordinary structure of the two-volume work made up of the Gospel of Luke and the Book of Acts illustrates this. Much of the last chapter of the gospel overlaps much of the first chapter of Acts. It appears that Luke, author of both, was trying to say that the life of Christ was introductory to the story of the church and that the story of the church was the fulfilment of the life of Christ. And, of course, Luke is at pains to demonstrate that the divine dynamic operant in and through the church was provided by the Holy Spirit. So, the Holy Spirit carries through the program initiated by God in Christ. This scenario finds echoes in Paul's writings.

It also introduces us to one of the great mysteries of the Christian faith—the relationship between God and the human person. There is an intimidating richness of images and analogies in Scripture related to this. To pick only one of these, Paul refers to believers in Christ as "temples," individually and corporately (1 Cor 3:16 and 6:19), and the language he uses in the original indicates "temple" in the sense of "holy of holies," a place where in some sense God the Holy Spirit actually "abides," to add a Johannine flavour. Believers are uniquely chosen sanctuaries. It is a staggering image of the relationship in question, if one stops and thinks about it.

The relationship is also transformational. In 2 Cor 3:17 and 18, Paul says,

> Now the Lord is the Spirit, and where the Spirit of the Lord is, there is freedom. And all of us, with unveiled faces, seeing the glory of the Lord as though reflected in a mirror, are being transformed into the same image from one degree of glory to another; for this comes from the Lord, the Spirit.

This is all part of Paul's well-known contrast between life in the Spirit and life in the flesh (Rom 6–8). The idea is that the Holy Spirit helps individual believers take on more and more of the characteristics of the divine nature. Of course, they remain humans, but they become more and more Christlike (see also 2 Pet 1:4). Gordon Fee catches perfectly the sense of this extraordinary intervention when he entitles his book on Paul's understanding of the Holy Spirit, *God's Empowering Presence.*

One dimension of this life "in the Spirit" is being led by the Spirit. Insofar as this Spirit is the all-knowing, all-wise, all-powerful God, being led by this Spirit is highly desirable. It could direct one to a richer, deeper, more significant, not to mention more God-pleasing, life. We see this in the experience of Jesus Christ himself. At the beginning of his ministry, we read, "Jesus, full of the Holy Spirit, returned from the Jordan and was led by the Spirit in the wilderness" (Luke 4:1). He couldn't miss what was intended for him; it was crystal clear. This directional involvement is also illustrated in the lives of the early followers of Christ. Luke, in Acts 16:6 and 7 writes,

> They went through the region of Phrygia and Galatia, having been forbidden by the Holy Spirit to speak the word in Asia. When they had come opposite Mysia, they attempted to go into Bithynia, but the Spirit of Jesus did not allow them; . . .

Again, there was no mistaking the divine wishes. We are not told how they received this information, but receive it they did.

There are two passages in which the idea is applied directly to Christians. The first is Rom 8:14 (led by the Spirit of God) and the second, Gal 5:18 (led by the Spirit). We are to understand that the agent in both cases is the Holy Spirit. To develop the discussion further, I note that being led by the Spirit is paralleled, in Paul's writing, by two other expressions: "walk in the Spirit" (eg., Rom 6:4; 8:4; Gal 5:16, and 4:1) and "guided by the Spirit" (Gal 5:25). The usual context is a discussion of the ethical life and specifically the tension between life lived according to the wishes of the Spirit and life lived according to the preferences of the flesh. Whatever the contexts, it is comforting to think that one might receive that kind of specific and infallible direction from God.

So, what can we, individuals or churches, expect from God's guidance, from being "led by the Spirit"? Can we know the mind of God with certainty? Can we rejoice in apparently divinely-certified novelty? Are there dangers here? Well, yes there are. We are always faced with plain, old subjectivity. I can be convinced that something is Spirit-led because it feels right to me, but is it? What makes it feel right? My personal perceptions of reality? How trustworthy are they? There is a documentable case in which someone convinced that he was led by the Spirit instructed his host to sell her piano and give the money to missions. When she broke into tears, he interpreted her upset as disobedience. Sobbing, she explained that she couldn't sell the piano—it belonged to someone else.

Back in the early 90s, Trent University culture critic Andrew Wernick could be heard arguing that the whole of public discourse was saturated with the drive to promote, with the attempt to sell things. He would also contend that our "promotional culture" was terribly deficient in good faith. Wernick had good grounds for these opinions and he was not alone in holding them. We live in a world where increasingly everyone is trying to manipulate everyone else for her/his own benefit. So maybe the impression that we think is the Spirit's leading is just the result of somebody's doing an effective selling job on us. Perhaps the "nudge of the Spirit" is ideologically-rooted arousal stimulated by sit-coms or commercials or billboards. Is there a way out of this box beyond robust suspicion of everybody and everything? Can I never know what the Spirit's leading actually is? Happily, I can. There is a standard.

JESUS CHRIST AND THE LEADING OF THE SPIRIT

Some quotations:
Rowan Williams, Archbishop of Canterbury:

> "The sign of Spirit is the existence of Christlikeness (being God's child) in the world."[8]

James Dunn, recently retired Professor of Divinity, Durham University:

> "The character of the Christ event is the hallmark of the Spirit."[9]

Gordon Fee, recently retired Professor of New Testament, Regent College:

> " . . . Christ is the absolute criterion for what is truly Spirit activity."[10]

Dunn again:

> "What is implied (in biblical passages which he has been studying) . . . is that the Spirit of God, hitherto a somewhat nebulous concept,

was now being understood as related to Christ. Jesus Christ had come to be seen as the definition of the Spirit."[11]

Williams, Dunn, and Fee are acknowledging the link which is found in Scripture between Jesus and the Holy Spirit. The Holy Spirit does not function independently of Christ. Everything that the Holy Spirit does focuses attention upon Christ, is governed and controlled by God's revelation of himself in Christ, and conforms to the teaching and practices of Christ. This leads me to a principle with regard to the leading of the Spirit: *to be led by the Spirit is to be drawn closer to Jesus Christ and into a deeper degree of Christlikeness.*

This should not be surprising, given what the Gospel of John shows us about the working of the Holy Spirit. Three passages in all of which Jesus is speaking:

> But the Advocate, the Holy Spirit, whom the Father will send in my name, will teach you everything, and remind you of all that I have said to you. (John 14:26)

> When the Advocate comes, whom I will send to you from the Father, the Spirit of truth who comes from the Father, he will testify on my behalf. (John 15:26)

> He (the Spirit) will glorify me, because he will take what is mine and declare it to you. (John 16:14)

Representative of the many comments which scholars have made on these passages are the following: "The teaching of the Holy Spirit recalls what Jesus has said, taking it deeper and farther into the memory and consciousness of the disciples of Jesus during the in-between-times;"[12] ". . . the Paraclete will enable the disciples to see the full meaning of Jesus' words."[13]

The scripturally-revealed purposes and work of the Holy Spirit are inextricably tied to Christ. The Holy Spirit does not function outside of the parameters of the life and teaching of Jesus, and for good reason. Jesus's life and teaching were the clearest possible revelation of the character, the love, the grace of God, so by clarifying and drawing attention to Christ the Holy Spirit is completing the circle of God's self-disclosure. Wolfhart Pannenberg has much to say on this.[14]

Finally, then, if we want to achieve some confidence about what we think might be the leading of the Spirit, we have a criterion: *whatever is the leading of the Spirit will glorify Christ and conform to the life and teaching of Christ.* That, of course, leaves us with the responsibility of being as well-informed as possible regarding the life and teaching of Christ. That, in turn, directs us to the Bible, requiring serious, well-instructed study applying the best tools and methods possible. There is virtually no other place in which we can learn about Christ than the Bible and meditation upon it. Now we can restate the criterion: *whatever is "leading of the Spirit" will glorify Christ and conform to the life and teaching of Christ as they are revealed in Scripture.* We cannot function only on subjective impressions. We must not be captured by ideologically-driven agendas from any direction. Impressions and agendas must be evaluated over against what the Scriptures teach us of Christ.

And when we examine the Scriptures with regard to homosexuality, we discover that, in fact, Jesus did make a statement that bears on the subject. The question turns on the meaning of the Greek word *porneia*. Of course there is debate among scholars.[15] However, Friedrich Hauck and Siegfried Schulz writing in the epochal *Theological Dictionary of the New Testament* (published in English in 1968, but available in German much earlier),[16] Jacques Dupont in 1959,[17] James Dunn in 1998[18], and David Janzen in 2000,[19] to name only a representative sample, have reached a widely-held consensus. The word is general in scope and refers to all kinds of sexual intercourse outside the marriage of a woman and a man. In Matt 15:19 and 20, and its parallel Mark 7:21, Jesus lists *porneia* among behaviours which defile a person, and, obviously, such defilement is to be avoided.

CONCLUSION

There can be no doubt that being led by the Spirit is highly desirable for all Christians. Paul urges us to walk in the Spirit and to be guided by the Spirit. Being led by the Spirit would avoid many false steps and provide much pleasure to God. However, the idea of being led by the Spirit must never be separated from Christ. Spirit guidance does not refer to an ephemeral, inchoate, will-o'-the-wispish sensation or emotion. It refers to Christ. To be sure that one is being led by the Spirit, one does not shut oneself into a room to agonize in isolation nor does one retreat into conventicles of like-minded people hoping for the reinforcement of one's dreams. Indeed, one brings the impressions gained in prayer or fasting or meditation or elsewhere and submits them to those who are more mature in the faith. But most importantly, one brings them to the Scriptures where the purposes of God and the will of Christ are revealed, and one makes one's submission to what one finds there. The leading of the Spirit never moves one away from the Christ of the Scriptures.

NOTES

1. "An Urgent Request for Your Support—The 2008 Canterbury Campaign, On the Road to Inclusive Communion," Integrity. www.integrityusa. org/CanterburyCampaign/index.htm. (Accessed May 16, 2008).

2. Aaron McCarroll Gallegos, "Where the Spirit Moves," *Sojourners Magazine* 37 (2008): 12-15.

3. James H. Kroeger, M. M. "Led by the Spirit into the Paschal Mystery," *Missions Studies* 10 (1992): 236-240.

4. Thomas Williams, "God Who Sows the Seed and Gives the Growth: Anslem's Theology of the Holy Spirit," *Anglican Theological Review* 89 (2007): 611- 627.

5. Philip Jenkins, *The Next Christendom: The Coming of Global Christianity* (Oxford: University Press, 2002), 8.

6. Matthew P. Lawson, "The Holy Spirit as Conscience Collective," *Sociology of Religion* 60 (1999): 341, n.1

7. Douglas John Hall, "'The Great War' and the Theologians," in *The*

Twentieth Century: A Theological Overview (ed. Gregory Baum; Ottawa: Novalis, 1999), 7.

8. *On Christian Theology* (Oxford: Blackwell, 2000), 124.

9. *Jesus and the Spirit: A Study of the Religious and Charismatic Experience of Jesus and the First Christians as Reflected in the New Testament* (London: SCM, 1975), 321.

10. *God's Empowering Presence: The Holy Spirit in Paul's Letters* (Peabody, MA: Hendrickson, 1994), 837.

11. *The Theology of Paul the Apostle* (Grand Rapids: William B. Eerdmans, 1998), 263.

12. Francis J. Moloney, S. D. B., *The Gospel of John* (Collegeville: The Liturgical Press, 1998), 413.

13. Raymond E. Brown, S. S., *The Gospel According to John* (xiii-xxi), Vol. 29A in The Anchor Bible; (New York: Doubleday, 1970), 650.

14. *Systematic Theology* (trans. Geoffrey W. Bromiley; Grand Rapids: William B. Eerdmans, 1991), 1.300ff., especially 315.

15. For example—the suggestion that the word refers to consanguinity: J. A. Fitzmyer says "yes" ("Matthean Divorce Texts and Some New Palestinian Evidence," *Theological Studies* 37 [1976]: 197-226) and Augustine Stock says "no" ("Matthean Divorce Texts and Some New Palistinian Evidence," *Biblical Theology Bulletin* 8 (1978): 24-33). The text in question is 11Q Temple Scrolla (11Q19 [11QTa]) in Florentino Garcia Martinez, *The Dead Sea Scrolls Translated: The Qumran Texts in English* (trans. W. G. E. Watson; 2nd ed.; Grand Rapids: Eerdmans, 1996), Col. LVII, p. 174.

16. "πόρνη," VI, 579ff.

17. *Mariage et divorce dan l'évangile: Matthieu 19, 3-12 et parallèles* (Abbaye de Saint-André : Desclée de Brouwer, 1959), 106.

18. Dunn, *The Theology of Paul*, 121.

19. "The Meaning of *porneia* in Matthew 5.32 and 19.9: An Approach from the Study of Ancient New Eastern Culture," *Journal for the Study of the New Testament* 80 (2000): 68–88, esp. 68 and 79. To this list could be added J. A. Fitzmeyer, "Matthean Divorce Texts," 208, Joseph Jensen, "Does *porneia* Mean Fornication?" *Novum Testamentum* 20 (1978): 161–184, esp. 179ff. and Marcus Bockmuel, "Matthew 5:32; 19:9 in the Light of Pre-Rabbinic Halakhah," *New Testament Studies* 35 (1989): 291–95, esp. 294f.

ANNOTATED BIBLIOGRAPHY

Dunn, James D. G. *Jesus and the Spirit. A Study of the Religious and Charismatic Experience of Jesus and the First Christians as Reflected in the New Testament.* London: SCM, 1975.

Dunn retired recently as Professor of Divinity at Durham University. He has had an extraordinary career as a New Testement exegete with numerous articles, monographs, and biblical commentaries to his credit. The book cited above, although published early in his career illustrates the perspicuity and erudition of his work. It also demonstrates his spiritual sensitivity. In particular, his treatment of the the Pauline "gifts of the Spirit" is perhaps the best to be found in the scores of books at which I have looked.

Fee, Gordon D. *God's Empowering Presence: The Holy Spirit in the Letters of Paul.* Peabody, MA: Hendrickson, 1994.

Having launched his career with a book on Papyrus Bodmer II (p66), Fee proceeded to produce excellent work both as a commentator and a biblical theologian. This book is a model of the genre, bringing text criticism, exegesis and spiritual acuity together against a background of exhaustive familiarity with the relevant literature.

SECTION THREE

Culture and Gospel

Chapter Seven

Contextual Exegesis in Africa
and the Anglican Crisis

Grant LeMarquand

I t has been noted repeatedly that the present crisis within Anglicanism over the issues of same-sex blessings and the ordination of those in same-sex relationships is partly the result of dissimilar views of the Bible. It is obvious to most observers that so-called "conservative" Anglicans and so-called "liberal" Anglicans view the Scriptures differently because they come to the text with differing theological assumptions. This essay will explore an issue raised less frequently, but it is one which is not often enough examined; that is, that there are cultural as well as theological differences at play when one reads (or hears) the biblical text. Everyone reads from a particular perspective. It does imply that my experience, the experience of being a man or a woman, a Canadian or Peruvian, English-speaking or Yoruba-speaking will colour my understanding.

The question of how cultural context affects our ability to understand biblical texts is implied in a recent article by the Presiding Bishop of the Episcopal Church which appeared, following Lambeth 2008, in several British newspapers. She wrote,

> . . . forms and structures of the various provinces of the Anglican communion [sic: Communion] have diverged significantly, in ways

that challenge those ancient ties to England and the Archbishop of Canterbury. Those provinces are the result of evangelism tied to colonial structures, whether of Britain or her former colonies, and that colonial history has still to be unpacked and assessed.[1]

In other words, the Communion is now global and the emergence of this global family of churches took place in the context of the colonization of the non-western world by western powers. In various ways "evangelism [was] tied to colonial structures" during the period of the British Empire and, I might add, during a period of history in which American power began to spread around the globe.[2]

Various inferences can be drawn from Dr. Jefferts Schori's observation of the post-colonial nature of our present context for theology and biblical exegesis. One might be led to ask, for example, if what is meant is that the present crisis of Anglicanism is simply the result of the accident of history in which the majority of missionaries who spread the Anglican version of Christianity in Africa, Asia and Latin America were of a theologically conservative (either evangelical or Anglo-Catholic) variety. One might further say (and I have heard it said) that these missionaries tended to be rather "pre-critical" in their views of Scripture and therefore their converts are of like mind. The assumption behind this line of thought is that non-western people are something of a *tabula rasa,* a blank slate on which the missionaries were able to inscribe their own theological views which were then appropriated by the "natives" uncritically. In other words, it might be possible to read the Presiding Bishop's words (and I am not saying that she actually meant this) as implying that the "colonial structures" and "colonial history" of the mission enterprise were such that evangelism in the colonial period virtually guaranteed that non-western Anglicans would be conservative in their theological views.

The problem in the Communion, therefore, is not really the fault of these non-western Anglicans, since all they did was believe what the white missionaries told them, and (unfortunately for the Africans, Asians and Latin Americans) they got the wrong kinds of missionaries.

Instead of broad church, more liberal-minded missionaries, they got the narrower, conservative type. I wish that I could say at this point that I am painting a caricature or holding up a straw man. Sadly this line of reasoning is heard repeatedly and in less subtle forms than in the quotation above. A protest must be made against the assumption that non-western Christians are unthinking and uncritical and have simply appropriated the Christian faith brought to them without question, as if they were clones of the white missionaries who brought them the gospel.

Neither can it be assumed that the evangelism of the late eighteenth to the early twentieth centuries, as compromised and ambiguous as it may have been, was entirely enmeshed in the colonial project. True enough, many missionaries were unaware of their own cultural biases. Missionaries and mission organizations too often assumed that "Christianity, civilization and commerce" went together and that the way to reach non-western people with the gospel was first to give them the benefits of western civilization. And it is true that many missionaries benefited from and supported the colonial systems with which they were inevitably identified. On the other hand, many missionaries advocated on behalf of the local people and worked against unjust structures that exploited them.[3] Along with the obligation felt to preach the saving message of Jesus Christ, the missionaries (especially British missionaries) of the colonial period were motivated by a desire to reverse the horrific effects of the slave trade and to somehow repay Africa for the terrible damage done by that exploitation. Indeed the very idea of "Christianity, civilization and commerce" that now makes us cringe was based on the longing to replace the abusive commerce of the slave trade with some more legitimate enterprises that might be of benefit to those being colonized. Hindsight reveals how fleeting some of those hopes actually were. However that may be, the assumption that mission work of the nineteenth century was simply the arm of Empire is too simplistic.

Behind the rhetorical link made between white missionaries and colonialism is the idea that Christianity is really only a western religion after all, so that its spread across the continents was really a regrettable mistake. Indians already had Hinduism and Buddhism, the Chinese already had Buddhism and Confucianism, First Nations people already had a perfectly good religion of their own, and so forth. Sadly, it is said, along with the colonial project Christians brought their western religion and forced it on non-western peoples. The idea of Christianity as a religion of the West seems to be deeply inscribed in our thinking and in our institutions. Many religion departments in secular universities divide their curriculum into two parts—East (Asian religions like Hinduism and Buddhism), and West (Judaism and Christianity). Many western Anglicans even feel a kind of guilt for having imposed "our" religion on non-western people, so much so that a service was held recently in one American diocese in which an apology was given to all Hindus that Christian evangelism had attempted to convert them.[4] If evangelical and Anglo-Catholic missionaries had left well enough alone, the Anglican Communion would be comfortably white and western and we would not need to live through the conflict we are now in. But of course, Christianity is not western, although it has lived and thrived in the western world for two millennia.

A Variety of Anglican African Bible Readers

Now we come to the substance of this essay. As I noted at the outset, it is sometimes said that the problem that Anglicanism is living through is partly a problem of biblical interpretation. I have been a part of many conversations in which it is said, with some sadness, "if only they [usually 'they' in these contexts means African Christians who disagree with the more liberalizing decisions concerning sexuality in the North American churches] had access to the best of biblical scholarship on this issue." The implication of this sentiment seems to be that if these Africans did have access to the "best scholarship" they would naturally agree with the western liberalizing decisions about sexuality. Even worse, perhaps, the assumption left unstated is that Africans have had no legitimate and fruitful ways of reading the Bible for themselves. And so, this essay offers merely a taste of how a few African Anglican biblical scholars, preachers and ordinary Christians "read" the Bible. I focus on Africa, partly because it is the part of the non-western world that I know best, but also because it is the part of the Anglican world which has (I think) been most misunderstood and denigrated in the current Anglican debate.

To the best of my knowledge, the first doctoral thesis in biblical studies earned by an African writing in English was John S. Mbiti's[5] 1963 Cambridge dissertation, "Christian Eschatology in Relation to Evangelisation of Tribal Africa" which was later published as *New Testament Eschatology in an African Background.*[6] It is important to take note of Mbiti's methodology. Although the degree which he earned was in New Testament studies and his supervisor was the eminent New Testament scholar C. F. D. Moule, Mbiti also acknowledges the insight and help which he received from G. I. Jones, an anthropologist, and Bishop Lesslie Newbigin, a missiologist and long time bishop in India. Mbiti's study was unusual because he foregrounded a pastoral problem as the context of his biblical research. In the world of biblical studies dominated in the West by the quest for objectivity rather than relevance, by the uncovering of past history rather than present meaning, Mbiti's work was radical.

The issue which Mbiti explored was the disjunction between African culture and the western cultural Christianity of those who evangelized his home area of Ukambani in Kenya, as well as the disjunction between African culture and the Bible itself. The presenting problem was what Mbiti perceived to be the differences between the concept of time in the New Testament, the futuristic eschatology of the teaching of the Africa Inland Mission (a dispensationalist theology stressing the second coming of Christ, the millennium, and the rapture) among the Akamba and what Mbiti took to be the African conception of time. He argued that the New Testament occupies a middle ground between the concept of time of the missionaries, which is vertical and future-oriented, and the more horizontal and present-oriented concept of African thought.

Mbiti has been criticized on a number of grounds, particularly for seeming to imply that Africans have little or no concept of the future, and for generalizing from Akamba ideas to Africa in general. But whatever criticism of his work may or may not be valid, the fact remains that his method of reading the New Testament with one eye on the context of the first century and one eye on the African missionary and cultural contexts was seminal for African exegesis.

Another Anglican New Testament scholar, John S. Pobee from Ghana, published his *Persecution and Martyrdom in the Theology of Paul* in 1985.[7] Although the African context is nowhere mentioned explicitly in the text of Pobee's book, it is clear that he had his eye on the African situation. In his preface, Pobee outlines the reason for his choice of topic: "Though a happy and privileged sojourner in Cambridge, my heart was bleeding for my motherland, Ghana, which had come into the grip of a corrupt and ruthless tyrant and government. While I laboured to follow my calling as a New Testament scholar, I also agonized over the fate of loved ones back home, my parents and the Church of God."[8] Mbiti's thesis highlighted the missionary and cultural context; Pobee's the context of suffering in a post-colonial world. Both seemed to sense that the task of biblical exegesis was incomplete without making a link between the biblical material and the context for which or out of which it is being read. By foregrounding the relevance of the biblical text to the African situation, both Mbiti and Pobee underline the fact that there is no exegesis without some kind of application.

Sammy Githuku, an Old Testament scholar from Kenya, has continued the tradition of examining biblical texts in the light of African culture.[9] Githuku examines the verse in 2 Sam 24:1–10 and asks a question that few other readers have been able to answer effectively: "Why does David feel guilty for counting his soldiers?" Verse 10, for example, says that David's "conscience is stricken," that he admits his "sin," his "guilt," and his "foolishness" in taking this action of counting. Githuku argues that in his own culture (he is a Kikuyu from central Kenya) there are traditional taboos around counting livestock and even family members. He suggests that some similar taboo may have weighed on David's conscience.[10] If Githuku's reading is correct, Africa has helped us to read a text which would have been difficult to understand without Africa's help.

One of Githuku's colleagues in Limuru, Joseph Galgalo approaches the biblical text from the perspective of a systematic theologian. In a recent publication, facilitated and edited by Philip Groves of the Anglican Communion Office, a chapter is devoted to a discussion of "Christian Spirituality and Sexuality" between Galgalo and an American woman (Debbie Royals) who is self-identified as lesbian. It is clear from the outset that the two parties in the discussion have widely differing views.

For his part Galgalo is clear that the biblical story provides the framework for any theological or ethical discussion. He sees God as the creator, who has made all things good; he sees the origin of evil and brokenness in the world in the Fall. For him, therefore, sexuality is a good gift of God, but this gift has been distorted by sin. Surprisingly, Royals identifies this perspective as "western" and argues that Christian mission is not about restoring sinful human beings to a right relationship to their creator, but rather that "The Baptismal Covenant [of the 1979 Episcopal prayerbook] becomes the definition of mission—focusing on justice and peace, the dignity of every human person and our willingness to reach beyond the barriers we have created to separate us from each other whether by race, class, sex, or any other wall."[11] Sexual practice, for Royals, is an issue of justice.

Galgalo disagrees:

> On the basis of 'being in the image of God,' I acknowledge that we all deserve to be treated with the dignity befitting one made in the image of God, and on this basis alone, accepted, loved and valued. We are not in dispute over justice here. If I may ask, however, must sex be part of the package for me to be truly seen to accept and love another human being? I find it hard to accept the nuance that one must express the acceptance and love of God for the other through indiscriminate sexual relationships or expressions.[12]

Galgalo goes on to assert that his view of sexuality is not "western," but both African and biblical:

> Most traditional cultures, such as my own African culture, have a

more positive view of sex and sexuality [than the ancient Platonic and Stoic views]. . . . They are a lot more similar...to views generally expressed in the Hebrew Bible, which forms the basis for Jesus' sexual ethics and morality as presented in the New Testament. The African traditional culture highly values human sexuality. . . . Sexual intercourse establishes marriage and procreation is a religious duty. Sexual pleasure and enjoyment is valued, although it is incidental to the act of procreation and strictly confined within the marriage covenant. . . . Anything else [i.e. any other type of sexual expression] contravenes the norm and is deemed as culturally inappropriate.[13]

It should be noted that Galgalo is discussing African culture here, but he considers this African perspective to be very close to the views found in the Hebrew Bible and the New Testament. In the end Galgalo concludes that he has gained much from the discussion, but comes away "more convinced than ever before that the basic contention between people on the different divide of this debate is fundamentally about the authority of Scripture."[14]

Of course the Bible is not just read by scholars. The Anglican ordinal (in any of its versions) exhorts preachers to expound the Scriptures. The Anglican catechetical tradition encourages all Christians to shape their lives by regular reading of the Bible. These lessons have not fallen on deaf ears in the so-called "younger" churches of the global south.

One example of an African preacher who has attempted to expound the Scriptures faithfully in the midst of a situation of political conflict is the former Archbishop of Kenya, David Gitari. During a period of political tension in Kenya, Gitari often preached expository biblical sermons that also addressed the public life of the nation. Because of his courage in speaking out Gitari's life was often in danger. In June of 1987, for example, Gitari (while bishop of Mt. Kenya East) preached a sermon at a church in Nyeri District in which he compared the Kenyan situation to the situation of Daniel in Daniel 6. Daniel was a faithful civil servant who, when faced with a choice between obeying a corrupt and unjust government for which he worked, found it necessary to obey God rather than that unjust structure. Gitari exhorted the politicians and civil servants in the congregation to remember that their first duty was to God, not to any human being or political system. The Kenyan press reported on Gitari's sermon in the Monday papers. The Tuesday papers were full of criticisms of the bishop by Kenyan politicians, one of whom accused the bishop of using "irrelevant" biblical texts for political reasons. The next Sunday (June 23, 1987), Gitari preached on 2 Tim 3:14–4:7 and highlighted that there are no "irrelevant" texts in Scripture, that "all Scripture is inspired by God and profitable for teaching, for reproof, correction and for training in righteousness" and it is the job of the preacher to preach the message of the Bible even if it is unpopular. "The churches," the bishop said, "have constantly and patiently to make clear that the gospel of Jesus Christ is concerned about every aspect of human life—intellectual, physical, spiritual and social."[15]

In his desire to unveil the social and political dimensions of the biblical text, Archbishop Gitari bears much resemblance to Desmond Tutu, former Archbishop of South Africa, who bravely appealed to the liberating dimensions of the biblical text within the racist apartheid regime of South Africa. Tutu's writings are voluminous.[16] In a context in which the Bible was used as a weapon of racial oppression by racist readers, Tutu argued that interpretations of the Bible that led to conclusions that white people were superior to black people were illegitimate interpretations which abused the biblical text. The Bible, according to Tutu, was a liberating text.[17] Tutu's view of the Bible as having a liberating trajectory, his strong view of human beings created in the image of God, and his belief that those who identify themselves as homosexual are also oppressed has in recent years led Tutu to the conclusion that the Bible is on the side of those who advocate for blessing same-sex unions and ordaining practicing homosexuals.[18]

How Scripture is read and put into practice by ordinary Christian people is a subject which requires further research and study. A few examples of so-called "popular" readings of Scripture in Latin America and other contexts have been published.[19] Several analyses of African "popular readings" are also available.[20] Of special interest is the study of the impact of Scripture Union on Christian communities in West

Africa by the Anglican New Testament scholar Andrew Igenoza.[21] Igenoza argues that in Nigeria and Ghana the desire for an escape from poverty, healing from sickness, deliverance from evil spirits, and many other practical needs for security and protection have shaped the questions that most Christians bring to the biblical text. Igenoza studies the way that the organization Scripture Union has addressed these practical needs. Present in West Africa since 1890, in the 1960s the organization de-centralized, allowing each national group to form its own indigenous identity. The Nigerian and Ghanaian movements took this opportunity to produce notes for private and group Bible study which included discussion of local religious issues such as witchcraft and occult beliefs.

Although the West African context became a clear focus of Scripture Union in West Africa, principles of biblical interpretation which were distinctly inherited from the Protestant Reformation formed the matrix in which these local problems were addressed. For example, Scripture was to be read as a whole. If Bible readers come across a passage of Scripture which is hard to understand, they should read that passage in the light of those which are more readily understood: Scripture interprets Scripture.[22] The Bible is not considered a source for proof texts, but rather a story with a clear Christological focus. The Bible is a narrative which leads to the story of the fulfillment of God's purposes for the world in the life, death and resurrection of Jesus Christ. Neither is the Bible seen as an ahistorical set of ideas: it was written in particular times and places and so the proper interpreter of the Scriptures must take the original intent of any passage into account. At the same time, the Bible is God's book, and since it was inspired by the Holy Spirit, the Holy Spirit is needed for it to be properly interpreted and applied. Readers, therefore, should always pray for God's guidance when reading the Bible.

Igenoza argues that these interpretative principles, together with a keen attention to the West African context, has made Scripture Union one of the most effective lay organizations providing Christian formation in Ghana and Nigeria across denominations, but including Anglicans.

Conclusion

This short survey has shown that there are certainly a variety of approaches taken towards the Bible by Anglicans in Africa. African biblical scholars have not jettisoned western exegetical methodology, but most have found the western tools to be lacking in relevance and application. African preachers have certainly not confined their preaching to what in the West would be considered the "religious" or "spiritual" spheres. Since all of life—devotional, sexual, political, social—must come under the Lordship of Christ, the Bible must be used to instruct and exhort in a holistic way. Certainly ordinary Christians in Africa, as anywhere, sometimes read the Bible literalistically or simplistically or even magically, but most read the text devotionally asking for the guidance of the Spirit and wrestling with the text to find its proper application in their lives.

An obvious weakness of contextual approaches, such as those outlined above, is that they can sometimes emphasize the context in which the text is read in such a way that the context in which the text was originally written can become submerged. There can, therefore, be a danger of reading one's own concerns into the text, rather than in light of the text. On the other hand, most contextual exegetes, while not abandoning the historical-critical methods of studying the Bible that have been developed in the West, will wish to remind us that this danger of eisegesis is just as real among those who attempt to tame and control the text using these historical-critical methods. No one comes to the text without a pre-understanding which in various ways shapes our conclusions.

Since the Anglican Congress in Toronto in 1963, the Communion has held up "mutual responsibility and interdependence in the Body of Christ" as an ideal to which Anglicanism should strive.[23] We have focused in this essay on contextual exegesis in Africa. Unfortunately, few outside of Africa have made a serious attempt to understand African theologians or African Christians. The turmoil of the present Anglican situation makes the ideal of "mutual responsibility and interdependence" appear to be a long way off. Sadly, in the current Anglican crisis African Christians have been stereotyped and scapegoated.[24] As one American church historian has noted, "The American and British church leadership, who had worked for three decades to promote an international Anglican consciousness, were unprepared for that consciousness to question them, and were inclined to blame the surge of the African bishops [at Lambeth 1998] on bribery by North American dissidents (or, in more bleakly racist terms, on African primitivism.)"[25] One way to combat stereotypes is to get to know the "other" as a real person. It is my hope that this short review has given readers a glimpse into one little bit of the intersection between the Bible and Africa.

Notes

1. Katharine Jefferts Schori, "The Road from Lambeth," Online: http://www.guardian.co.uk/commentisfree/2008/aug/09/anglicanism.religion?gusrc=rss&feed=worldnews (Accessed August18, 2008)

2. The only comprehensive history of the Anglican Communion is that of Kevin Ward, *A History of Global Anglicanism* (Cambridge: CUP, 2006); the global spread of Anglicanism in the context of American spheres of influence and the notion of "manifest destiny" has been analyzed by Ian Douglas in *Fling out the Banner! The National Church Ideal and the Foreign Mission of the Episcopal Church* (New York: The Church Hymnal Corporation, 1996); no thorough study of Canadian mission work has yet appeared, but for an example see Darren Marks, "'Against the Goads:' The Beginnings and Formation of the Canadian Diocese of Mid-Japan (1888–1935)," in *Anglican and Episcopal History* 75/4 (1995): 442–58.

3. Examples could be multiplied, but see for the Kenya context Gideon Githiga, *The Church as the Bulwark Against Authoritarianism: Development of Church and State in Kenya with Particular Reference to the Years After Political Independence, 1963–1992* (Oxford: Regnum, 2002).

4. Connie Kang, "Service celebrates 2 beliefs" January 20, 2008, print edition B-3. I have not been able to find out what the bishops of the churches in India think of this apology to Hindus for evangelizing them. Would they now believe that they ought to give up the Christian faith and return to practicing Hinduism?

5. Mbiti is an Anglican priest from Kenya.

6. *New Testament Eschatology in an African Background: A Study of the Encounter between New Testament Theology and African Traditional Concepts* (London: Oxford, 1971).

7. Pobee also studied at Cambridge. The dissertation was published in the University of Sheffield's Journal for the Study of the New Testament Supplement Series (number 6).

8. *Pobee, Persecution and Martyrdom,* vii.

9. Githuku has taught Old Testament at St. Paul's United Theological College (now St Paul's University) for more than a decade. He is a graduate of St. Paul's, but has a Canadian connection, having completed an M.A. in Old Testament at McGill. He has recently completed doctoral studies at the Catholic University of East Africa, possibly the first non-Roman Catholic to do so.

10. "Taboos on Counting," in *Interpreting the Old Testament in Africa: Papers from the International Symposium on Africa and the Old Testament in Nairobi, October 1999* (ed. Mary Getui, Knut Holter and Victor Zinkuratire; New York: Peter Lang / Nairobi: Acton, 2001), 113–17.

11. Joseph Galgalo and Debbie Royals, "Christian Spirituality and Sexuality," in *The Anglican Communion and Homosexuality: A resource to enable listening and dialogue* (ed. Philip Groves; London: SPCK, 2008), 239-265, here 242.

12. Ibid. 244.

13. Ibid. 255. On page 258 Galgalo includes "incest, cross-generational and cross-gender" sexual expression as practices which African culture and the Bible would both consider to be contraventions of the norm.

14. Ibid. 265.

15. David Gitari, *Let the Bishop Speak* (Nairobi: Uzima Press, 1988), 48. Cf. Gitari, *In Season and Out of Season: Sermons to a Nation* (Carlisle: Regnum, 1996) and John Karanja, "The Biblical, Prophetic Ministries of Henry Okullu and David Gitari," *Anglican and Episcopal History* 75/4 (2006): 58–604.

16. The best bibliographical listing is probably Michael Battle's *Reconciliation: The Ubuntu Theology of Desmond Tutu* (Cleveland: Pilgrim Press, 1997).

17. Tutu's opinion, shared by many "liberationist" interpreters in South Africa, as well as Latin America, came under severe criticism by Itumeleng J. Mosala, who argued that the Bible is not in fact a liberating text and that the Bible itself was in need of liberating. See his *Biblical Hermeneutics and Black Theology in South Africa* (Grand Rapids: Eerdmans, 1989).

18. A question must be raised here about whether the issues of race and

sexual orientation are equivalent or even analogous. Being black (or white. . .) is not a behavior.

19. See Ernesto Cardenal, *The Gospel in Solentiname* (3 vols; Maryknoll: Orbis, 1982). Cf. the examples in R.S. Sugirtharajah, ed. *Voices from the Margin: Interpreting the Bible in the Third World* (new edition; Maryknoll: Orbis, 1995), Part Five, "People as Exegetes: Popular Readings."

20. See especially, Gerald West, *Contextual Bible Study* (Pietermaritzburg: Cluster, 1993); idem, *The Academy of the Poor: Towards a Dialogical Reading of the Bible* (Sheffield: Sheffield Academic Press, 1999); Justin Ukpong, "Popular Readings of the Bible in Africa and Implications for Academic Readings: Report on the Field Research Carried out on Oral Interpretation of the Bible in Port Harcourt Metropolis, Nigeria under the Auspices of the Bible in Africa Project, 1991-1994," in *The Bible in Africa: Transactions, Trajectories and Trends* (ed. Gerald West and Musa Dube; Leiden: Brill, 2000), pp. 582-94; David Adamo, *Reading and Interpreting the Bible in African Indigenous Churches* (Eugene: Wipf and Stock, 2001); Grant LeMarquand, "Bibles, Crosses, Guns and Oil: Sudanese 'Readings' of the Bible in the Midst of Civil War," *Anglican and Episcopal History* 75/4 (2006): 553-79.

21. Andrew Olu Igenoza, "Contextual Balancing of Scripture with Scripture: Scripture Union in Nigeria and Ghana," in West and Dube, 292–310.

22. This is very similar to the principle found in Article XX of the XXXIX Articles, that "it is not lawful for the Church to ordain any thing that is contrary to God's Word written, neither may it so expound one place of Scripture, that it be repugnant to another."

23. See "Mutual Responsibility and Interdependence in the Body of Christ: A Message from the Primates and Metropolitans of the Anglican Communion," in *Anglican Congress 1963: Report of Proceedings* (ed. Eugene Fairweather; Toronto: Anglican Book Centre, 1963), 117–22.

24. See my essay "African Responses to New Hampshire and New Westminster: An Address" in *Anglican and Episcopal History* 75/1 (2006): 13–36.

25. Allen C. Guelzo, "Bonfire of the Sacristies: To the 2006 General Convention" *Anglican and Episcopal History* 75/1 (2006): 98–118, here 111–12.

CHAPTER EIGHT

WORDS DO NOT STAND STILL

Not Even Anglican Ones

Roseanne Kydd

ABSTRACT

This paper will focus on the grammar and meaning of two questions from General Synod 2007 addressed to the Primate's Theological Commission via the Primate, the Most Rev. Fred Hiltz. The Canadian Anglican context of these questions is the dispute between two groups over the reception of same sex unions in the Church. Lambeth 1.10 has ruled in favour of the sanctity of exclusive male/female marriage and the Canadian General Synod 2004 has ruled in favour of the sanctity of same-sex unions. While same-sex unions are the presenting issue, the debate is much deeper, raising matters of procedure, authority, ecclesiology, doctrine, pastoral care, tradition and change. The unity of the Anglican Church of Canada and the whole Anglican Communion is at stake. It is my purpose to critically evaluate these questions which participate in this Communion dispute to assure maximum clarity in their structure and wording. My assumption is that questions with such wide-ranging ramifications must be free of ambiguity and bias, and agreed upon by the principal parties involved.

INTRODUCTION

God puts great stock in words and language. Indeed the great capacity for speech is an outstanding mark of humanity. The first chapter of John's Gospel expresses the culmination of God's longing to reveal himself to his creatures, the Incarnation: "And the Word became flesh and lived among us." Christ as the Word is God's answer to the forked-tongue serpent whose words beguile and deceive.

The twentieth century has seen the rise of a new focus upon words and the operations of language, described variously as a rhetorical turn, discourse analysis, cognitive linguistics, or the popular "double speak." The *Journal of Language and Politics* epitomizes this shift, noting the basic assumption "that the *language of politics* cannot be separated from the *politics of language*." In American politics each party accuses the other of manipulating language. One Republican blogger writes, "Few areas of left wing perversion have been more successful than the conscious manipulation of language for ideological purposes." On the other side, Democrat George Lakoff, professor of cognitive linguistics at the University of California, Berkeley, and founder of the progressive think tank, the Rockridge Institute, has made headlines with his foregrounding of the mechanisms of conservative political catch phrases using the concept of "framing." He charges that Republicans owe their success to having defined the language structures. Each party races to outdo the other in mastering double-speak.

Lakoff points to the example of gay marriage as a conservative rallying topic. By using "marriage" as the frame, the concepts of "marriage is about sex" and "gay sexuality" are collapsed, obscuring the more fundamental agreement among conservatives and liberals that none wishes to discriminate against gays. Homophobia seems not to be the issue. Lakoff proposes making the issue "freedom to marry" or "the right to marry." "Very few people would say they did not support the right to marry who (*sic*) you choose. But the polls don't ask that question, because the right wing has framed that issue," says Lakoff. The fact that Lakoff himself is attempting to manipulate language to favour his own progressive agenda, by obscuring the sexual nature of gay distinctiveness and of marriage, escapes him. Surely a criterion for fair debate, as opposed to a calculating discourse that deliberately hides parameters, includes putting all the issues onto the table. Transparency is important—if not perfectly achievable—when truth matters more than winning.

Is language ever neutral? Can't we just "Say it like it is"? Recognizing that words carry historical and political traces, that their meanings change over time and exhibit a certain fluidity, it does not follow that all propositional varieties are equal. Clarity of expression is a legitimate goal and failures in clarity have proved serious in many instances. Even the most radical devotees of word play (or dancing Derridian *différence*) would acknowledge the importance of clear syntax under certain circumstances.

I offer the following question on Quebec sovereignty to illustrate the seriousness of word choice and sentence structure, and the wide ramifications of not constructing a statement whose clarity was agreed upon by the principal contenders in the debate. This example may strike one as over-inflated in comparison with our Anglican dispute over same-sex blessings. But think for a moment: the population of Quebec in round figures is 8 million in a country of 33 million. The population of the global Anglican Communion is estimated at 80 million in over 160 countries. Decisions made in our small corner affect more Christians worldwide than Quebec's vote affects Canadians in Canada.

On October 30, 1995 a second referendum was held in Quebec to decide if the province should secede from Canada and become an independent state. The small margin of rejection, 50.58% to 49.42% was a wake-up call for Canadians. Many protested on the "No" side that the question itself was unclear. The Clarity Act grew out of this objection, was passed by the Liberal government and became law on June 29, 2000. Some would describe the redefinition of marriage within the church as a social and religious phenomenon on a scale larger than the secession of a national province. Consider the excerpt from the Clarity Act in light of the questions we as Anglicans pose for decision-making:

> WHEREAS any proposal relating to the break-up of a democratic state is a matter of the utmost gravity and is of fundamental importance to all of its citizens;
>
> WHEREAS the Supreme Court of Canada has determined that the result of a referendum on the secession of a province from Canada *must be free of ambiguity both in terms of the question asked and in terms of the support it achieves . . .*
>
> WHEREAS the Supreme Court of Canada has stated *that democracy means more than simple majority rule, . . .* and that a *qualitative evaluation is required to determine whether a clear majority in favour of secession exists in the circumstances;*
>
> House of Commons to consider question
> (1) The House of Commons shall, . . . *consider the question and, by resolution, set out its determination on whether the question is clear.*
>
> No negotiations if question not clear
> (6) The Government of Canada shall not enter into negotiations . . . if the House of Commons determines, . . . *that a referendum question is not clear and, for that reason, would not result in a clear expression of the will of the population of that province on whether the province should cease to be part of Canada.* [my emphasis]

The thrust of this Act was to ensure that all sides of the matter were convinced of the clarity and fairness of the question. This would require debate in the House of Commons and Senate where both sides of the dispute were represented. In light of the gravity of the situation facing the Anglican church, the clarity of the language of the questions being considered becomes paramount. I will examine the Primate's two questions under three headings: 1. Syntax, 2. History and 3. Critical Analysis.

I. SYNTAX OF THE QUESTIONS

In stressing "clarity" it is useful to recognize this term as a figure of speech. "Clarity" is a metaphor drawn from the sighted eye, stressing the eye's capacity for visual sharpness and focus.

Some of its qualities are borrowed to express the mental "clarity" of other fields, like concepts, and language.

The following formulations were presented for consideration to the Primate's Theological Commission by the 2007 General Synod:

> 1. *the theological question whether the blessing of same-sex unions is a faithful, Spirit-led development of Christian doctrine;*
>
> 2. *Scripture's witness to the integrity of every human person and the question of the sanctity of human relationships.*

Both are sentence fragments labeled "questions," yet they are neither interrogative (one meaning of "question") nor in the formal structure of resolutions—"Be it resolved that . . ." (another meaning of "question"). Assuming that a grammatically-correct sentence would produce greater precision, I will create an indicative sentence by inserting the verb "is" after "question." A question, understood as something with an outcome to be determined, need not be in the interrogative form. However, putting it as a direct interrogation heightens the either/or aspect expected in the response, but here entails dropping "the theological question." It may be argued that "the theological question" is not a necessary part of the sentence where words like "Spirit-led," "Christian," and "doctrine" connote discussion related to God. (Later I will pursue some implications for categorizing this question as a theological one.) The sentences will look like this:

INDICATIVE SENTENCE: The theological question is whether the blessing of same-sex unions is a faithful, Spirit-led development of Christian doctrine.

INTERROGATIVE SENTENCE: Is the blessing of same-sex unions a faithful, Spirit-led development of Christian doctrine?

In the second fragment, the quickest means to a sentence is to change the first two words, "Scripture's witness" to "Scripture witnesses." A problem immediately becomes apparent: what is questioned—whether Scripture does witness to the integrity of every human person and so on—turns into an affirmative statement. Introducing "the theological question" might prevent turning what is under question into a statement. As these are the Primate's Questions for the Theological Commission, let's make it into an interrogative question. A further modification removes "the question of the" to allow the parallelism of two prepositional phrases "to the integrity of" and "to the sanctity of" to balance each other. Inserting "the question of the" interferes with the clearer association of "integrity" and "sanctity." Here are the modified sentences:

INDICATIVE SENTENCE with parallel structure: The theological question is whether Scripture witnesses to the integrity of every human person and to the sanctity of human relationships.

ALTERNATIVELY: The theological question concerns/addresses/raises Scripture's witness to the integrity of every human person and to the sanctity of human relationships. (Here what is at stake is assumed, that Scripture *does* witness to the integrity of every human person and to the sanctity of human relationship.)

INTERROGATIVE SENTENCE with parallel structure: Does Scripture witness to the integrity of every human person and to the sanctity of human relationships?

Each of the adjusted sentences states with greater clarity what is being questioned. The alternative one epitomizes the problem of circular reasoning—assuming as statement what is under question—and therefore must be rejected. The interrogative form more faithfully reflects the claim that these are questions to be answered. Insofar as a question is open-ended, an answer can be fairly expected in a positive or negative mode. Thus the word "whether" implies "or not" in the sentence. This addition would acknowledge more readily the possibility of the "either/or" expectation as built into the asking mechanism. "Whether/or not" matches "either/or" and expects "yes or no."

However, this probing reveals yet another meaning embedded in the question: What is Scripture's witness with regard to the ideas of "the integrity of every human person" and "the sanctity of human relationships"? This formulation avoids both circular reasoning and the greater expectation of an affirmative answer that comes with omitting "or not."

II. HISTORICAL TRAJECTORY OF QUESTIONS

The awkwardness of these two formulations raises some queries. Where did they come from and why these formats? Is there something in the history of these questions that justifies maintaining them in their present form?

1. The St. Michael Report

The General Synod [GS] of 2004, St. Catherines, Ontario, requested of the then Primate, the Most Rev. Andrew Hutchison, that he direct a question to the Primate's Theological Commission "whether the blessing of committed same-sex unions is a matter of doctrine." With the Rt. Rev. Victoria Matthews as chair, the St. Michael Report concluded that the blessing of same-sex unions is a matter of doctrine, but is not core doctrine in the sense of being creedal. The latter became resolution A186 and was passed by GS in 2007, Winnipeg.

2. A Statement to the Anglican Church of Canada from the Primate's Theological Commission [PTC]

A number of the resolutions presented by the Council of General Synod identified the resolutions with the St. Michael Report. This *Statement*, issued by PTC, was a correction to that error. It was only the first question above that became a GS resolution. The *Statement* highlighted two matters of importance:

The first is cited in the last sentence of the Report and succinctly states the doctrinal issue before the Anglican Church of Canada:

"It is now for the Church to decide whether or not the blessing of same-sex unions is a faithful, Spirit-led development of Christian doctrine."

In its report the Commission has drawn attention to a range of theological and biblical matters relating to how the Church determines whether such a matter is "a faithful Spirit led development of Christian doctrine."

The second is a pair of questions from paragraph 16 of the Report. These questions are of similar theological significance to the life of the Anglican Church of Canada as the doctrinal issue itself:

"Is it theologically and doctrinally responsible for one member church of the Communion to approve a course of action which it has reason to believe may be destructive of the unity of the Communion?

"Is it theologically and doctrinally responsible to accept unity as the value which transcends all others, and therefore for a member church of the Communion to refrain from making a decision when it believes it has an urgent gospel mandate to proceed?"

The commissioners believe that these questions should be considered by the church, and most certainly by delegates to General Synod prior to General Synod's discernment and determination on these matters.

3. Bishops' Pastoral Letter

The next setting for the re-appearance of this first question is the Bishops' Pastoral statement (May 1, 2007) intended to go to General Synod 2007.

Looking ahead, we ask the Primate and General Synod for a report on:

1. The theological question whether the blessing of same-sex unions is a faithful, Spirit-led development of Christian doctrine (St. Michael Report)

2. The implications of the blessing of same-sex unions and/or marriage for our church and the Communion (The Windsor Report)

3. Scripture's witness to the integrity of every human person and the question of the sanctity of human relationships.

We ask that this report be available in advance of General Synod 2010.

We commit to taking this ongoing conversation to the Lambeth Conference 2008.

4. New Primate's Theological Commission

At the conclusion of the General Synod of the Anglican Church of Canada held in Winnipeg in June 2007, the Primate, Most Rev. Fred Hiltz, was asked to refer two matters to the Primate's Theological Commission for consideration:

1. the theological question whether the blessing of same-sex unions is a faithful, Spirit-led development of Christian doctrine;

2. Scripture's witness to the integrity of every human person and the question of the sanctity of human relationships.

The middle question from the Bishops' Letter, "The implications of the blessing of same-sex unions and/or marriage for our church and the Communion" was dropped. It seems the implications are very serious.

III. CRITICAL ANALYSIS OF THE DEVELOPING FORMULATIONS

Let us return to the first appearance of question one for the PTC 2007 from page 113:

1. *the theological question whether the blessing of same-sex unions is a faithful, Spirit-led development of Christian doctrine*

and compare it with its source in *A Statement to the Anglican Church of Canada from the Primate's Theological Commission*:

"It is now for the Church to decide *whether* or not *the blessing of same-sex unions is a faithful, Spirit-led development of Christian doctrine*" [my emphasis].

Only the italicized words remained in the new Primate's Theological Commission question. What implications might flow from these adjustments?

1. *First Adjustment*: The elimination of "It is now for the Church to decide" has been replaced with "the theological question."

a. A difference in syntax occurs with a sentence fragment resulting from the substitution of "the theological question" for "It is now for the Church to decide." A full sentence is generally a vote for greater clarity. Either the original or the indicative sentence, "The theological question is whether the blessing of same-sex unions is a faithful, Spirit-led development of Christian doctrine" is preferred in this respect.

b. The deletion has the effect of narrowing the frame of reflection from an ecclesiastical category of "the church" to a theological one. While theoretically ecclesiology is a subset of theology, theology is itself a subset of the larger church, a discipline in its service. This ideal may no longer hold as the philosophical leanings have gained ground to produce an autonomous field. What ramifications does this movement from "the church" to "theology" entail?

i. The category of "church" is a broader one than that of theology. It suggests a process of democratizing involvement of laity, clergy, and scholars, including theologians. It diminishes the control of decision-making of professional bureaucratic elites and committees to include lay people on a wider scale. It expresses the inclusivity of the Anglican Church of Canada.

ii. The category of "church" can also suggest the ecumenical Christian church. Christian unity and our ecumenical partners are not a small consideration for Anglicans. The Chicago-Lambeth Quadrilateral states: "That in all things of human ordering or human choice, relating to modes of worship and discipline, or to traditional customs, this church is ready in the spirit of love and humility to forego all preferences of her own." Has the church changed its mind in this commitment?

iii. Having determined who is to be the agent, (the church), the words "now" and "to decide" convey some urgency in making a decision. The substitute, "the theological question" drains away any notion of urgency or need to decide.

iv. A movement away from "church" to "theology" runs the risk of privileging philosophy over exegesis, relegating the role of Scripture to a lesser one than is stated in Anglican historic documents including The Windsor Report. "Within Anglicanism, scripture has always been recognized as the Church's supreme authority, and as such ought to be seen as a focus and means of unity." (TWR 27 # 53)

2. *Second Adjustment*: The words "or not" have been removed from their source in the *Statement*. A more transparent question will keep the "or not" as a means of acknowledging the possibility of either a negative or positive response. (See earlier discussion under SYNTAX.)

So far I have zeroed in on the removal of phrases from the PTC 2004, the St. Michael Report, to the questions before us for the PTC 2007. There is another word that is less than satisfactory and that is the use of "Spirit" as in "Spirit-led." I would here want to add a word, and that is "Holy" to produce "Holy Spirit-led." My concern arises from widening connotations of the word "spirit" as it has entered a popular discourse of the last twenty years. Jeremy Carrette and Richard King have written a compelling book on the hidden business of spirituality: *Selling Spirituality: The Silent Takeover of Religion.*[1] The following collage of quotations amply illustrates the skepticism we ought to have with respect to a dangling "spirituality":

"'Spirituality' has no universal meaning and has always reflected political interests" (30). "There are perhaps few words in the modern English language as vague and woolly as the notion of 'spirituality'" (30). "With the establishment of psychology as the pre-eminent 'science of the self' in the post-war period, we see an increasingly 'non-religious' understanding of spirituality emerge. This changing climate within modern capitalist societies has led many traditions, including established western ones such as Christianity, to 'de-mythologise', by moving away from the older cosmological and disciplinary language of the past and replacing this with the interiorised and psychologically inflected language of 'spirituality'" (43). "Indeed, spirituality can be mixed with anything since, as a positive but largely vacuous cultural trope, it manages to imbue any product with a wholesome and life-affirming quality" (46). "Its vagueness and ambiguity allows it to mask the underlying ideologies that it is used to represent" (47). [Spirituality] "deflects criticism and obscures meaning" (49).

To recap this development: the movement of the first question from General Synod 2004 to the Primate's Theological Commission which produced the (1) St. Michael Report's conclusion, to a 2007 General Synod Resolution, its reappearance in the PTC's (2) Statement to the Anglican Church as a doctrinal issue before the AC of C, and then its incorporation directly into the (3) Bishop's Pastoral Letter to GS 2007. I copy them below for reference:

1. The theological question whether the blessing of same-sex unions is a faithful, Spirit-led development of Christian doctrine (St. Michael Report)

2. The implications of the blessing of same-sex unions and/ or marriage for our church and the Communion (The Windsor Report)

3. Scripture's witness to the integrity of every human person and the question of the sanctity of human relationships.

Here the first question of the Bishop's Letter is identical to the one directed to the Primate's Theological Commission 2007 with the modifications discussed above from its first appearance in the PTC 2004. The second question nods to the second set of questions from the PTC *Statement* above (on page 116) without spelling out the ends of the spectrum as the pair of questions from paragraph 16 does. Although this question along with its changes is of importance and cries for investigation, I will not address this disparity because it is not included in the two questions presented to the PTC 2007. The third question is the source of our second question, *Scripture's witness to the integrity of every human person and the question of the sanctity of human relationships.*

In streamlining question two on page 114 of this paper, I proposed removing "the question of" to make visible the parallel structure of the prepositional phrases. Is there any reason to preserve "the question of"? Where has "the question of the sanctity of human relationships" been raised before? It, too, has resonance with precedents, the removal of which might obscure this link. An amendment to a resolution from the General Synod of 2004 introduced by the Rev. Canon Garth Bulmer of the Diocese of Ottawa affirmed "the integrity and sanctity of committed adult same-sex relationships." Let us compare these two expressions more closely:

GS 2004	Affirms	the integrity and sanctity ➜	of committed adult same-sex relationships
Primate's Theological Commission 2007	[Confirms]	the integrity ➜	of every human person and
		the question of the sanctity of ➜	of human relationships

The earlier use of "integrity and sanctity" and "relationships" in the GS 2004 resolution acts as a frame for the PTC 2007 questions. By carrying over the structure and resonance of GS 2004, it raises the expectation/possibility that agreeing to the question may involve agreeing to the 2004 resolution, a still controversial statement. By virtue of its similarity to the former presentation, this statement muddles the discussion and the fair presentation of alternatives that an unsettled question normally assumes.

The repetition of the words "integrity," "sanctity," and "relationships" draws attention to them, in a sense "neon-ing" them as either positively or negatively charged on the basis of one's perspective. For the Lesbian, Gay, Bisexual, and Transgendered [LGBT] community, these are words of hope and encouragement; for those distressed by the haste of the resolution and this choice of words, these are untimely words precipitously determined. They serve to underscore tension and faulty procedure, emphasizing winning and losing rather than thoughtfulness and care.

Integrity

On the surface, "integrity" seems to trade on the language of human rights. Article 3 of the Charter of Fundamental Rights of the European Union 1999 affirms the "right to the integrity of the person." However, the use of "integrity" is also divergent from earlier rights traditions that underscore "dignity." The United Nations Universal Declaration of Human Rights, December 10, 1948, commences its Preamble with:

> Whereas recognition of the inherent *dignity* and of the equal and inalienable rights of all members of the human family is the foundation of freedom, justice and peace in the world,

> Article 1. All human beings are born free and equal in *dignity* and rights. [my emphasis]

Similarly, Vatican ll "declares that the right to religious freedom has its foundation in the very *dignity* of the human person, as this *dignity* is known through the revealed Word of God and by reason itself" [my emphasis]. In the context of Anglican debate, "integrity" is a freighted word, loaded and primed. It is not a new word, but it does have a relatively new vocation as the name of an activist group of LGBTs within the Anglican Communion. The LGBT advocates have been deft in the reclaiming of words. Their rescue of "gay" and "queer" from terms of abuse to labels of "pride" testify to great skill and determination. The word "pro-life" has a decided political meaning that has transcended any specific lobby group to designate those who are opposed to abortion. Its capturing of the vibrancy of "life" gives the progressive Rockridge Institute a bad case of envy. In a conference report from November 2005, one reads, "Re-claiming the mantle of pro-life may be our greatest task." When a word becomes so closely associated with one side of a deeply divisive issue, can the other side be expected to concur in statements coloured by the highly-charged words from one side of the debate? Can progressivists use "pro-life" apart from its current ownership by anti-abortionists? Similarly can those doubtful about Scripture's witness to same-sex blessing agree to propositions where "integrity" is a key term?

Sanctity

Sanctity is a four-piece Thrash Metal band from Asheville, North Carolina, USA, formed in 1998 and still active. They have released one album, *Road to Bloodshed*, on April 24, 2007, containing such pieces as "Road to Destruction" and "Beloved Killer." This is not the first meaning of "sanctity" that comes to mind, but words do slip and slide. The word is not typically part of the human rights discourse as are "dignity" and more recently "integrity." "The sanctity of life" slogan is prominent in pro-life and anti-euthanasia literature in advocacy for the unborn and the terminally ill. Its most common usage, however, stems from the religious realm. The *Catholic Encyclopedia* provides a succinct explication of sanctity:

The term "sanctity" is employed in somewhat different senses in
relation to God, to individual [persons], and to a corporate body.
As applied to God it denotes that absolute moral perfection which
is His by nature. In regard to [human beings] it signifies a close
union with God, together with the moral perfection resulting from
this union. Hence holiness is said to belong to God by essence, and
to creatures only by participation. Whatever sanctity they possess
comes to them as a Divine gift. As used of a society, the term
means: that this society aims at producing holiness in its members,
and is possessed of means capable of securing that result, and that
the lives of its members correspond, at least in some measure, with
the purpose of the society, and display a real, not a merely nominal
holiness. The Church has ever claimed that she, as a society, is holy
in a transcendent degree. She teaches that this is one of the four
"notes", viz., unity, catholicity, apostolicity, and sanctity, by which
the society founded by Christ can be readily distinguished from all
human institutions.

The Scriptures witness to the sanctity of God, the church, and Christians as participants in God's gift of holiness. I know of no obvious
biblical witness to *the integrity of every human person and the question
of the sanctity of human relationships*. It is much easier to locate Scripture's witness to the sinfulness of every human person (Rom 3:23)
and the perversity of relationships. Certainly if one substituted in the
sentence a word similar to integrity, like "righteousness," the results
would be even more unsatisfying. ("All our righteous deeds are like
a filthy cloth" [Isa 64:6]). It seems the traditional Christian sense of
worthiness, integrity, or wholeness stems primarily from participation
in the work of Christ, an act requiring personal decision coupled with
grace, epitomized in the sacraments of Baptism and Holy Communion.
The applying of "sanctity" as a description to human persons or relationships without qualification is at best dubious.

Relationships

There are relationships and there are relationships. What kind
of relationships is this question addressing? Until this is specified,

affirming the question is a bit like signing a blank cheque. More refinement is required here if clarity is to be achieved. Does Scripture witness to the integrity and sanctity of sibling relationships? From Cain and Abel to James and John, these relationships prove to be competitive and less than perfect or sanctified.

CONCLUSION

On the basis of the critical analysis of the two questions for consideration by the PTC in this paper, I will substitute this formulation for the first question:

> 1. Is the blessing of same-sex unions a faithful, Holy Spirit-led development of Christian doctrine or not?

For the second question, I can restructure it with clearer syntax: "What is Scripture's witness with regard to the ideas of 'the integrity of every human person' and 'the sanctity of human relationships'?" However, syntax does not solve the lack of transparency because of the problematic wording, plagued as it is with the hot terms "integrity" and "sanctity" along with the lack of specific meaning for "human relationships." Framing it as a theological question makes matters worse because of the overwhelming witness of Scripture to human fallenness and depravity apart from Christ. I fail to understand the significance of this question as it stands, apart from its being a dubious sequel to the GS 2004 resolution affirming "the integrity and sanctity of committed adult same-sex relationships." And if the idea presented in this question, with all its brimming connotations, is the only logical response and direction to take, it is badly flawed as a means of promoting honest investigation.

How we use language is important and it must be done with care, balance, and fairness. Ultimately, this debate is not about *language*. It is about *substance*. Language fails when it obscures the substance of the dispute and this is what has happened in the questions to the Primate's Theological Commission. We can do better and we should.

Jesus: "Let your word be 'Yes, Yes,' or 'No, No.'"

NOTES

1. Jeremy Carrette and Richard King, *Selling Spirituality: The Silent Take-over of Religion* (London: Routledge, 2005)

CHAPTER NINE

Anglicans in the Age
of Human Rights

George Egerton

When the 2007 General Synod asked the Primate's Theological Commission for guidance on whether "same-sex blessings is a faithful, Spirit-led development of Christian doctrine" and the question of "Scripture's witness to the integrity of the human person and the sanctity of human relationships," members of the Commission were faced with questions charged with cultural, moral, political and theological impact. Such words as "sanctity," "integrity," "blessings," "doctrine," "faithful," and "human person," are all freighted with theological and political import—not least in their intersection with related issues of human rights. What does "the integrity of the human person" mean? Where does it come from? What human relationships merit the religious affirmations of "sanctity" and "blessing"? How can we discern what is a "faithful, Spirit-led development of Christian doctrine"?

Canadian culture, along with much of Western Europe, has decided in political and court decisions to grant legal recognition to same-sex unions and marriages. The website of Integrity, the principal Canadian

IN SPIRIT AND IN TRUTH

Anglican LGBT (Lesbian, Gay, Bisexual, and Transgender/Transsexual) lobby, describes their mission as "a national network of organizations and friends working toward the full inclusion of gay and lesbian people in the life of the Anglican Church of Canada. We are part of the international lesbian and gay Christian movement, encouraging churches around the world to promote the basic human rights of gay and lesbian people and to support their active participation in the life of the Church." Who can oppose movements for "integrity," "basic human rights," and "full inclusion"? It seems no respectable Anglican would want to be caught on the wrong side of these words. But what constitutes a human right? Where do human rights come from? Are there any limitations to human rights? What do we do when rights conflict with other rights, or when they conflict with Christian teachings and doctrine? Have there been any studies within Anglicanism which address these dilemmas?

The present study is written with the conviction that dilemmas of human rights lie at the heart of the current travails of Canadian and world Anglicanism. It is hoped in this brief analysis to cast some historical light and understanding on how human rights have evolved in Anglican theology, especially as articulated through the Lambeth Conferences and in Canadian constitutional politics and jurisprudence, where the subventions of the national churches have afforded opportunity to contribute a distinctive voice. It may be that, in the current divisions of Canadian Anglicanism, the power of bishops, the politics of synods, and the rulings of civil courts will determine the course of events, as the Canadian church (along with The Episcopal Church in the United States) seems intent on walking apart from the global Anglican Communion. Meanwhile, the remnants of orthodox Canadian Anglicanism go underground for the long haul or seek protection and global realignment under alternative Primatial and Episcopal oversight. Perhaps a miracle of discernment and prudence can yet pull us back from the brink of national fragmentation and international schism.

A central feature of Canadian history since the mid-twentieth century has been "the rights revolution," the quest to articulate and give legal protection to human rights and fundamental freedoms. In many ways, as with other modern democracies, this struggle has become the country's defining metanarrative, giving identity, normative ideals, and purpose to Canadian nationhood and juris-prudence. With the memory of the Jewish holocaust as its deepest impetus, the human rights metanarrative presents a story of progress, of dark ages giving way to enlightenment, of villains and heroes, of struggles, setbacks, and eventual victory. The Canadian version of the narrative dramatizes the repressions of civil liberties under the War Measures Act during both World Wars, the legal proscription of the communist party after 1919, the expulsion of Japanese Canadians from the Pacific coast during World War II by the Liberal government of Mackenzie King, the Cold War persecution of suspected communist spies under Louis St. Laurent, King's Liberal successor, and the *grande noirceur* of Quebec Premier Maurice Duplessis' use of the Padlock Act against the enemies of Catholicism—mainly communists and Jehovah's Witnesses. The story then turns to recount the mobilization of civil libertarians in the late 1940s, the role of Canadian John Humphrey in drafting the 1948 Universal Declaration of Human Rights, the Supreme Court 1950s triumphs of McGill law professor Frank Scott against the Duplessis regime, the passage of the Canadian Bill of Rights by the Conservative Government of John Diefenbaker in 1960, and finally the entry into the age of human rights under Liberal Prime Minister Pierre Trudeau. After the brief villainy of invoking the War Measures Act to intimidate Quebec separatist terrorists in the 1970 October crisis, Trudeau led the process which culminated in the patriation from Britain of the Canadian Constitution of 1982 with its Charter of Rights and Freedoms.

Subsequently, the Charter would profoundly re-shape Canadian politics and law, as political, cultural, and legal elites, especially the Supreme Court, have used the Charter to give new normative direction to social ethics and jurisprudence. Canada now takes pride in viewing itself as an exemplar of human rights and multiculturalism—and many millions of dollars in public and private financing are being committed to construct a Museum of Human Rights in Winnipeg to memorialize the story of human rights.

Canadian religious communities have played important parts in the progress of human rights since 1945, not least in the cooperation of Anglican and Jewish leaders. Anglicans—like John Humphrey who piloted the drafting of the Universal Declaration of Human Rights, Senator Arthur Roebuck who led the cause of human rights within the Liberal Party from King to Trudeau, Professor Frank Scott of McGill University who won the key civil liberties cases of the 1950s and mentored Trudeau in the constitutional entrenchment of a Charter of Rights, and Anglican Conservative MP Gordon Fairweather, who served as the founding and long-term Chief Commissioner of the Canadian Human Rights Commission—all made signal contributions to the advance of human rights in Canada and internationally. The role of Primate Ted Scott in the struggle for recognition of First Nations' rights in Canada, and in championing human rights against South African apartheid, also won accolades for Canadian Anglicanism.

Nevertheless, the relationship of the Canadian national churches to the triumph of human rights has not been untroubled. Indeed, concurrent to the human rights revolution, the formerly privileged public status and functions of religion in Canada have been severely curtailed in recent decades, as churches have been politically marginalized and religious expression relegated to the private sphere in an increasingly hostile political culture of secularized pluralism. The central role that human rights jurisprudence has come to exercise in defining national identity and purpose has, in many ways, supplanted the previous role claimed by the churches as "the conscience of the state." The ascent of human rights has been hailed by many who embrace the liberal meta-narrative as a triumph over the repressions, discriminations, and irrationality of religion, liberating Canadians from the strictures of their Protestant or Catholic traditions. Yet the process of living in the age of human rights has evoked varying responses from Canadian churches—

ranging from the enthusiastic support of liberal Protestants and progressive Catholics to the skepticism and alarms of evangelicals and traditional Catholics when human rights and historic Christian teaching seemed to conflict, and demand discernment and hard choices.

Can some historical understanding help us with these dilemmas? Questions related to the relationship of human rights and religion were debated intensively, in Canada and internationally, by politicians, political philosophers, theologians, and church leaders, as part of the process leading to the passage of the Universal Declaration of Human Rights in 1948—a document which ushered in the "Age of Human Rights."[1] During World War II, as the Grand Alliance fought its way to victory over the Axis Powers, the theme of human rights increasingly drew the attention and support of church leaders and organizations, particularly after knowledge spread regarding the nature and scale of Nazi wartime atrocities and genocide. The Vatican reaffirmed classic Catholic doctrine on the divine origin of state authority and the necessary right to religious freedoms, while denouncing the idolatry of totalitarian regimes. In 1942 the renowned French Catholic scholar, Jacques Maritain, a familiar figure in Canadian Catholicism through his frequent residence at the Pontifical Institute in Toronto, published *Les Droits de L'Homme et la Loi Naturelle*, undergirding his widely-translated and influential appeal for protection of human rights with an extensive neo-Thomist foundation in natural law. Maritain's central themes were that human "dignity" derived from God's creation of mankind "in His image"—the Catholic doctrine of *imago Dei*—and that human rights had their grounding in natural law as written in the hearts of all peoples.

Human rights and civil liberties received their most extensive theological articulation in wartime Canada when, after two years of cross-country consultations, the United Church published in 1944 a report on "Church, Nation and World Order." In this detailed and encompassing charter of "basic principles of a truly Christian civilization," church leaders attempted to present a political, economic, and social agenda for post-war Canadian domestic and foreign policies, confident in offering "guidance to the nation and to the world." "The Report" endorsed the maintenance of "traditional civil liberties" in an improved parliamentary system. Its extensive section on "The Duties and Rights of Man" specified rights to an abundant life, to justice, to personal freedom, to solidarity and community, to productive and gainful work, to a voice in government, to worship, to knowledge, recreation and leisure. Such rights, however, were "not absolute," and found meaning only in the context of reciprocal duties and responsibilities—as taught in the Christian maxim to treat others as one would want to be treated oneself. The report was explicit in its political theology: "The enduring foundation of social order is the moral law of God, to whom men and nations must give account, and whose will is that all His children should live as brothers. The personal dignity of man is derived from his worth in God's sight, and the social order must recognize this dignity."

Anglican thinking on human rights received thorough study when, in the summer of 1948, Anglican bishops from around the world met in London for the first post-war Lambeth Conference. Here, in denouncing the cruelties and false doctrines of the recently-defeated totalitarian states and the new menace of Stalinist Communism, the bishops put forward as their first subject, "The Christian Doctrine of Man." This doctrine alone could serve as the foundation for human rights:

> The conference declares that all men, irrespective of race or colour,
> are equally the objects of God's love and are called to love and
> serve Him. All men are made in His image; for all Christ died;
> and to all there is made the offer of eternal life. Every individual
> is therefore bound by duties towards God and towards other men,
> and has certain rights without the enjoyment of which he cannot
> freely perform those duties. These rights should be declared by the
> Church, recognized by the State, and safeguarded by international
> law.

The Lambeth Resolutions then endorsed the efforts of the United Nations to protect human rights, most especially the right to freedom of religious belief, practice, and education.

Later in the summer, the inaugural meeting of the World Council of Churches at Amsterdam put its support firmly behind the international protection of human rights in a manifestly theological grounding:

> The Church has always demanded freedom to obey God rather than man. We affirm that all men are equal in the sight of God and that the rights of men derive directly from their status as the children of God. It is presumptuous for the state to assume that it can grant or deny fundamental human rights. It is for the state to embody these rights in its own legal system and to ensure their observance in practice.

While the major international Protestant and Catholic statements had each articulated a theology of human rights, none of them had called for an explicitly confessional, Christian reference to serve as the foundation or preamble for a Declaration which was to be "universal," inclusive of the plurality of UN members' religions, and respecting the freedoms, as well, of the non-religious. Indeed, by this time leading Protestant and Catholic spokesmen had addressed the problem of pluralism, and conceded that however they defined the origin and justification of human rights within their own confessions, they could not expect to impose this on those subscribing to a universal charter. They made it clear, however, that the rights in a universal charter would have to be "acceptable from the Christian standpoint."

Canada would vote to accept the Universal Declaration of Human Rights at the UN General Assembly in December 1948. But the country's entry into the age of human rights was somewhat reluctant. The Liberal Government of Mackenzie King had misgivings as to what the adhesion to human rights instruments would mean to Canada's inheritance of the constitutional doctrine of Parliamentary supremacy, as well as the Provincial jurisdiction over "property and civil rights." Quebec Catholic leaders, in Parliament and Church, were concerned that human rights could be misused to diminish religious freedoms while promoting communism and irreligion. The policy syntheses that were articulated at this time entailed the following cardinal themes:

- the Canadian state was conceived as a "Christian democracy" where the pluralism of the Christian churches and liberal ideology guided the state cooperatively in its political, legal and cultural norms.

- Canada would support human rights instruments as part of its liberal polity and Christian conscience.

- human rights would be manifestly legitimated under the rubric of the dignity of the human person, which in turn derived from the theology of the person as created in the image of God— *imago Dei.*

These themes would be remarkably durable, from the 1940s until the constitutional watershed of 1982. Whenever there was movement in Canadian politics to expand the purview of rights, most notably to adopt a Canadian Bill of Rights, politicians, even more than church leaders, insisted that rights be subsumed under a theological referent. Catholic leaders remained most insistent on this—as when the 1960 Canadian Bill of Rights was passed,[2] Catholics Davie Fulton and Paul Martin Sr. representing the Progressive Conservative and Liberal parties cooperated in writing the Bill's Preamble:

> The Parliament of Canada, affirming that the Canadian Nation is founded upon principles that acknowledge the supremacy of God, the dignity and worth of the human person and the position of the family in a society of free men and free institutions . . .

The supremacy of God would not fare too well in the turbulent politics of the 1960s, as Canada celebrated its 100th anniversary in 1967 and invited the world to join the festivities at Montreal's Expo '67. While the Liberal Government of Lester Pearson welcomed the full participation of Canada's diversifying religious communities in an expanding religious pluralism, the national churches experienced severe demographic and cultural retrenchment through these years—most dramatically in the implosion of Catholicism in Quebec's quiet revolution. Concurrently, human rights, freedoms, and claims to equality flourished in Canada and across the border in the American civil rights movement. The churches struggled to understand and respond to the many challenges and changes being encountered. Vatican II (1962–65) stands as the most comprehensive and systematic ecclesial discernment and "aggiornamento;" Canadian Anglicans had to make do with the enthusiasm of Toronto's World Anglican Congress of 1963. The 1965 best-seller book, *The Comfortable Pew*, by then journalist and lapsed Anglican Pierre Berton, broke all Canadian sales records and engaged the mainline Canadian Protestantism in a firestorm of self-criticism and an urgent quest for renewed relevance. By brilliantly popularizing the main themes of pop-theologians like Bishop John Robinson, Berton captured and projected the agenda of Canadian liberal Protestants for the rest of the 20th century as they abandoned the old theology, the old curricula, and the old morality and embraced the new age of the pill, situation ethics, mass entertainment, and human rights. Berton was also the first major Canadian voice to advocate the expansion of human rights to include homosexual relations.

As the politics of human rights accelerated in Canada through the 1960s and 1970s, feminists, aboriginals, multiculturalists, Québécois separatists, and gay liberationists all mobilized to challenge the cultural, legal, and constitutional status quo. The traditional role of religion in Canadian political culture would undergo radical alteration. Canadian elites, especially in academia, law, and media, sensed that the churches' previous role as conscience of the state would have to be discarded if the new norms of liberation and rights were to achieve political acceptance. Nowhere was this more true than in the realms of family and marriage law and sexual ethics.

Central to the re-imagining of a new liberal Canada was the changing conceptualization of pluralism. Whereas Canadian pluralism had traditionally represented a fusion of its liberal parliamentary and Christian foundations, expanded by the 1960s to include other religious communities, Canadian elites now propounded that separation of church and state (as allegedly normative in American jurisprudence) was necessary to redefine Canadian pluralism, with religion being "privatized," its public status and functions suppressed. This deep cultural and constitutional shifting would find brilliant expression in the political career of Pierre Trudeau.

Trudeau, love him or hate him, stands as the primal political leader in re-imagining and legislating a liberal secular jurisprudence for modern Canada.[3] Haunted by his ultra-Catholic, corporatist socialization by the Quebec Jesuits, which led to his involvement in adolescent separatist plotting in WWII, and then converted at Harvard from this personal *grande noirceur* to an equally doctrinaire version of Anglo-American liberalism, Trudeau would serve as Canada's philosopher-king, as character and circumstance combined in his transformative political career. With Duplessis' Quebec always a troubling memory for the architects of *Cité Libre*, Trudeau as Justice Minister in 1967 announced to Parliament the foundations of a new secularist Canadian pluralism and jurisprudence which would serve to guide legal reform:

> We are now living in a social climate in which people are beginning
> to realize, perhaps for the first time in the history of this country,
> that we are not entitled to impose the concepts which belong to a
> sacred society upon a civil or profane society. The concepts of the
> civil society in which we live are pluralistic, and I think this parlia-
> ment realizes that it would be a mistake for us to try to legislate into
> this society concepts which belong to a theological or sacred order.

It would be this political and legal theory, articulated recently in Britain's Wolfenden Report and American Supreme Court rulings on "strict separation" of church and state, which would guide Trudeau as Justice Minister and Prime Minister through the modernization and secularization of the Criminal Code, to remove the religiously-grounded proscriptions on birth control, divorce, therapeutic abortion, and homosexual relations.

As Trudeau also legislated official bilingualism and multicultural-ism, facing down the menace of Quebec separatism, Liberal govern-ments put the quest for protection and expansion of human rights at the centre of their political vision, as Canada adhered to the International Covenants on Economic, Social and Cultural Rights, and Civil and Political Rights, and in 1977 launched the Canadian Human Rights Commission with Gordon Fairweather as founding Chief Commissioner. It was clear that in refashioning Canada's legal system Trudeau and his Government saw the new regime of multiculturalism and human rights in secularist terms, where multiculturalism was defined in ethnic and linguistic terms, and where religion was excluded as a constituent component. Nor were the churches or religious communities to have any public or privileged function in giving moral directives. Rather, as with Trudeau's personal Catholicism, religion was to be privatized in a political culture of secularist pluralism. Anglicans most politically involved in this transformation were generally supportive: Senator Roebuck had been bemused by Quebec's neo-Thomist Catholic Senators and was happy to guide the new divorce legislation through Parliament; Frank Scott found the reference in the Canadian Bill of Rights to the supremacy of God "offensive." Gordon Fairweather was eager to expand the reach and mission of the Human Rights Commission without any public articulation of a theology of human rights. Submissions by Canadian mainline Protestant churches to Parliamentary committees studying morally charged questions generally favoured Trudeau's progressive legal reforms without concern for traditional Christian moral teachings.

When it came to the constitutional watershed of 1982 and the patriation of the British North America Act from Britain, with the Charter of Rights and Freedoms forming the first part of the Constitution Act of 1982, the preference of Trudeau and his Government for a secularist instrument ran into the powerful opposition of the Conservatives, articulated by the Mennonite Jake Epp, who insisted that a reference to the supremacy of God be inserted in the preamble to the Charter to pair with "the rule of law" and thereby reflect Canada's traditional religious and democratic condominium. In appearances before the Hays-Joyal constitutional committee, the United and Anglican churches championed the cause of human rights, the United Church Moderator advocating the inclusion of "sexual orientation" as a specified category of protection against discrimination. Anglican Primate Ted Scott focused on the human rights claims of First Nations, but when asked if the Charter needed a religious referent he responded by restating classic theology of *imago Dei* but recorded that this was not church policy, only his personal conviction.

The Charter of Rights and Freedoms would include a religious referent in its Preamble: "Whereas Canada is founded upon principles that recognize the supremacy of God and the rule of law . . ." This amendment resulted from the collaboration of evangelicals and Catholics who lobbied successfully and captured effective political support within the major political parties. The Evangelical Fellowship of Canada put the case most cogently in lobbying the Prime Minister:

> The acknowledgment of one Supreme God to whom we as a nation are answerable gives ground for legislation bearing on all matters human. To omit any such reference only leaves the door open for substitution of other less worthy grounds—utilitarianism, naturalism, secularism, etc.—since legislation cannot escape growing out of presuppositions. Moreover, human rights though recognized by the state in a democratic society are a sacred endowment from God not bestowed but administered by the state.

In the era of Charter politics and jurisprudence, as the purview of human rights has been expanded by activist courts and Human Rights Commissions, and as LGBT sexual identities and behavior have achieved constitutional recognition, including the right to same-sex marriage, Canada's oldline Protestant churches have generally accommodated the moral revolution involved in these departures. Leading advocates within Anglicanism of this transformation, notably the revisionist Bishop of New Westminster, Michael Ingham, have marched in the parade of human rights seemingly without any critical theology of rights and without a sense of what should result when ever-expanding rights claims collide with the moral teachings of the One Holy, Catholic, and Apostolic Church. In beating the drum of LGBT rights, Dr. Ingham has been as theologically derelict as he has been rhetorically and politically adept in leading his Diocese and the House of Bishops into the fold of human rights and religious pluralism. Nowhere in Canadian Anglicanism, it seems, have the array of study guides, dialogues, and synod position papers addressed theologically and systematically the areas where human rights expansions trespass upon classic Christian teachings. Only in evangelical Protestantism and in the magisterium of Roman Catholicism has this dilemma been addressed clearly and faithfully. Where international Anglicanism has articulated a clear theology of human rights, as in the Lambeth Conference of 1948 and then with utter clarity at Lambeth 1998, reaffirming classic and ecumenical teaching on human sexuality and marriage while proscribing homosexual behavior, unions and ordinations, the Anglican Church of Canada has forgotten, ignored, or subverted its own conciliar magisterium—claiming the revisionist freedom to innovate and choose "local options." In doing this it has not only done violence to the global Anglican Communion, it has replicated the sin of Eden in eating from the tree of the knowledge of good and evil, appropriating what belongs to God. The bitter fruit is a riven communion and a schismatic, sectarian Anglican Church of Canada, walking apart from the global Anglican Communion and classic Christian doctrines, as we find ourselves increasingly irrelevant in a post-Christian culture.

The Archbishop of Canterbury, Rowan Williams, in May 2008 delivered a profound address on "Religious Faith and Human Rights," demonstrating how Christian theology can provide more secure foundations for "embodied" human rights than secular rationales, which seem incapable of discerning between universal rights and an ever-expanding list of entitlements claiming the status of rights. Archbishop Williams did not address the divisions within the Anglican Communion deriving from just this phenomenon; but when pressed by revisionist Bishops at Lambeth 2008 to help move the Anglican Communion forward to keep up with western cultures and governments who have affirmed and legislated same-sex marriage under the rubric of human rights, the Archbishop wisely advised that any changes would have to come from within the church and its theology.[4] Human rights claims did not trump theology. Let us hope that Anglicans can pay heed to Archbishop Williams' discerning counsel.

NOTES

1. See the author's "Entering the Age of Human Rights: Politics, Religion, and Canadian Liberalism: 1945-1950," *Canadian Historical Review* 85.3 (September 2004): 451–479.

2. See the author's "Writing the Canadian Bill Of Rights: Religion, Politics, and the Challenge of Pluralism, 1957–1960," *Canadian Journal of Law and Society* 19.2 (December 2004): 1–22.

3. See the author's "Trudeau, God and the Canadian Constitution: Religion, Human Rights, and Government Authority in the Making of the 1982 Constitution" in *Rethinking Church, State, and Modernity* (ed. David Lyon and Margurite Van Die; Toronto: University of Toronto Press, 2000), 90–112.

4. See Rowan Williams "Religious Faith and Human Rights," 1 May 2008, and press interview of 3 August 2008: Online <http://www.archbishopof-canterbury.org>.

Scripture, Integrity and Sanctity

CHAPTER TEN

A Doctrinal Debate in Search of a Doctrinal Proposal

F. Dean Mercer

In the church's debate about same-sex relationships, there are two developments from General Synod 2007 and the questions put to the Primate.

First, "same-sex blessings" have now been recognized as a matter of doctrine, though of what kind remains unclear.

Secondly, and consequently, any further developments will require a proposed teaching, or doctrine, regarding same-sex blessings. No such proposal exists. Instead, only an assumed proposal and rationale appeared, now to be studied by the Primate in terms of "spirit-led development" and "Scripture's witness to the integrity of every human person."

In other words, and going back to GS 2007, no proposed doctrine or teaching regarding same-sex relationships has been presented or put forward for General Synod to examine. This is a serious omission, but it also throws into question the meaning of General Synod's conclusion that same-sex blessings do not conflict with the church's core doctrine.

The confusion was expressed within days of GS 2007's end. Bishop Tony Burton of Saskatchewan wrote that the church had done no more than state the obvious: "same-sex blessings are not in the creeds."[1] Rev. Alan Perry, an expert on canon law from the Diocese of Montreal, was quoted in the *Anglican Journal* (Aug 20, 2007) as saying "there is nothing in the church's canons or constitution that prevents a diocese from going forward with same-sex blessings now that General Synod has said it would not be against core doctrine."

Ask the chair of the St. Michael Report, Bishop Victoria Matthews, and you get a mediating conclusion, but one implying a great deal more work to be done than advocates have concluded: "GS 2007 distinguished the subject of same-sex blessings as a matter that is not a given of the faith. It is possible for change to occur. But the church is still waiting for the proposal that justifies the change" (Interview on New Zealand radio, March, 2008).

Before that, though, there is still the curious introduction of a novel category of "core doctrine." Appearing as it first did in the controversial Righter trial,[2] it has been criticized as a hollowing out of doctrine and an attempt to separate doctrine from ethics. A number of scholars have picked up on this:

> . . . the notion of "core doctrine" used to justify the [Righter trial] court's decision seems on the face of it to mean two things—one is that heresy is now a notion that cannot be brought into play; and the other is that moral matters are in no way matters of doctrine. "Core doctrine" as used by the jury in the Righter trial, refers only to the bare outline of the apostolic preaching as sketched by C. H. Dodd in 1935. Gone is the full scope of the biblical witness that once was thought to establish doctrine. Further, according to the panel of bishops who gave the judgment, even the thin reed of "core doctrine" must be interpreted within its "contemporary context." In all cases of conflict between "core doctrine" and the "contemporary context" it appears to be the "contemporary context" that wins out. In short, doctrine is gone and in its place there has appeared a Babel of theological opinion, none of which is privileged unless those who support a particular theological fashion are in power. If they are,

they inevitably find themselves under pressure to use their position to insure that only those who share their theological views are allowed in an effective way into the councils of the church. In this way, no need arises to speak of "the doctrine of the church." Those in power need only refer to the presently fashionable theology that serves to justify the interests of people who have like minds to themselves.[3]

As Philip Turner notes, the new category of "core doctrine" looks suspiciously like an end-run around the church's moral and ethical tradition by creating a strictly creedal category of doctrine which is received as a given (but, from the ruminations of some bishops, may be interpreted any way one wants), and an ethical and practical category which is relative, situational and local. In all of this, it should be noted that if General Synod's use of "core doctrine" meant what it did at the Righter trial, that is as novel within the Anglican Communion as any proposal for same-sex blessings.

The traditional distinction has been that between things necessary to be believed and those things which are indifferent—*adiaphora*. The Windsor Report dealt with this at length, including ways in which the two are distinguished.[4] As Stephen Andrews noted, the St. Michael Report pointed to a distinction, but also insisted that same-sex blessings bear on central doctrines:

> The [St. Michael Report] rightly observes that an issue like same-sex unions, while not itself a matter of core doctrine, carries strong implications for central doctrines such as what it means for human beings to be made in the image of God, salvation and marriage. So it would be a serious misreading of the intent of the report to isolate the category of "core doctrine" and claim that because same-sex unions are not to be categorized as such, they are not important enough to require greater consensus in the Anglican Church's deliberations.[5]

That said, in the absence of any proposed teaching regarding same-sex relationships, who knows whether or not there is a supportive scriptural rationale? Most frustrating of all for those whose primary obligation is the defence of the church's Scripture and tradition—a defence that is the solemn vow of every priest and bishop of the church—who knows how to address it?

The appeal to "Scripture's witness" in the church's deliberation about same-sex blessings in relation to the doctrine of the church meets this obstacle: the method and process of reading Scripture in this debate is itself in disarray. To date, and in descending order, three general approaches to Scripture have characterized this debate.

First, there has been a considerable body of literature that has attempted a plain and forthright grappling with Scripture, convinced that Scripture must be grappled with and that a coherent biblical rationale exists. Some would admit that a full and developed rationale has not been presented, but the seeds of such a rationale exist. The general argument has been that explicit biblical condemnations of same-sex relationships are specific to the time, or have been misunderstood, or are subservient to other, more dominant scriptural principles.

It should be noted that all of these arguments have been forcefully refuted.[6] More important, proponents have yet to present a positive statement from Scripture in favour of same-sex relationships. That statement would either have to place itself within the scriptural argument about the creation of male and female and the purposes of marriage, or it would have to convincingly overturn the church's teaching in favour of an altogether new understanding of humans and human relationships.[7]

Secondly, there are those who have been arguing that Scripture is not the prime source of the church's ethical teaching. Rather, the church must look to the baptismal covenant or some other doctrinal base. This position diminishes Scripture in favour of a supposedly alternative Christian foundation. Walter Wink, otherwise an advocate of same-sex blessings, put the matter bluntly:

> Efforts to twist the text to mean what it clearly does not say are
> deplorable. Simply put, the Bible is negative toward same-sex

behaviour, and there is no getting around it. The issue is precisely what weight that judgment should have in the ethics of Christian life. [8]

So far as catholic teaching goes, however, this approach falsely separates Scripture, doctrine and ethics.

And thirdly, there are those who reject Scripture altogether in favour of secular standards such as United Nation manifestos or Supreme Court rulings. Causes like "justice" and "human rights" have become the rallying point for proponents of same-sex blessings. The assumption behind the argument from human rights is that the Bible, by treating homosexual practice as wrong, proves itself to be inequitable and thereby invalidates itself. So a secular notion of justice based in the concept of the autonomous individual trumps the biblical portrayal of justice working itself out in the creative and redemptive purpose of God. If the cause is untrue and unfaithful to the purposes of God, it cannot be just—the hard lesson learned by every king of Israel.

And while only a few blantantly attack the Scriptures which they publicly read and preach, such dismissals fuel the distaste and disregard of many of this generation's clergy for the establishment of a clear and coherent scriptural rationale.

Or, as Old Testament scholar Elizabeth Achtemeier sums up the matter:

> Because much of the church in this country no longer believes or expects to hear God speaking through its Scriptures, it therefore is not very Christian anymore. And, of course, the results in our mainline churches have been simply devastating.[9]

As it stands, the scriptural rationales used to support same-sex blessings contradict each other. The first recognizes the importance of Scripture and attempts to reconcile Scripture with a proposal in favour of same-sex relationships. The second diminishes Scripture in favour of a purportedly superior foundation, like doctrine or baptism, though falsely separating baptism and doctrine from Scripture. And the third rejects Scripture out of hand.

Complicating matters further is that these three contradictory rationales from Scripture are being applied to four very different and contradictory proposals.[10] They are worth a moment's pause:

1) same-sex blessings *but not* same-sex marriages, or,

2) same-sex blessings *and* same-sex marriages,[11] or,

3) same-sex marriages *but not* same-sex blessings, or,

4) whatever consenting adults agree to.[12]

The proposals for same-sex blessing, same-sex marriage or mutually consensual relations are themselves contradictory. Same-sex blessings are proposed because, it is said, they do not impinge upon the church's doctrine of marriage. Same-sex marriage is proposed because, it is said, "blessings" are a second-class category, marriage should be the right of every person and the traditional distinction between male and female is no longer relevant. Mutually consensual relationships are proposed, it is said, because the traditional definitions and disciplines are regarded as untrue and oppressive to a radical and novel vision of humanity and relationships.

Yet in spite of the contradictory purposes of these proposals, advocates work together. Why? It is difficult not to think that the motive is political: the language of blessing is milder than the language of marriage and does not obviously require a lengthy engagement with the church's teaching on marriage. It is an easier point to win in synod. The Council of General Synod admitted as much in preparation for General Synod. "Ignore integrity, consistency or contradictions," advocates say to themselves. "Same-sex blessings are an effective first step. Win the day on that one, demoralize and expel the opposition, then proceed. Marriage—and whatever else is required to serve the growing list of sexual categories—will easily follow."

Politically it has been a very effective strategy. But it leaves aside that which might be considered characteristic of, even essential to, a church that calls itself catholic and apostolic: it leaves aside a thoughtful engagement with the apostolic witness and the long tradition of Christian reflection on Scripture in relation to marriage. It leaves aside also the collegiality, the willingness to listen to the voice of the other in our communion, something that has always been one of Anglicanism's particular strengths.

In all of this, there are two crucial things to note.

First, these three general approaches to Scripture contradict each other and in too many cases betray a loss of trust and confidence in the scriptures. Secondly, the proposals for same-sex unions are also several and contradictory. While proponents of same-sex relationships in Canada often present themselves as a large, coherent and unified body, their strength is that of revolutionaries. They know what they oppose— the traditional definition of marriage and the disciplines which flow from it. But they have not been at all clear about what they propose in its place or the reasons for doing so.

There are plenty of individual proposals and personal opinions. But the project that has been undertaken in Canada is the overthrow of one part of the catholic tradition and the scriptural rationale which supports it. The proposal of a consistent, non-contradictory, and hardy alternative is what is called for—and, to date, that is what has been entirely lacking. What we have instead is an assortment of contradictory proposals and rationales.

But secondly, and finally, in the absence of concrete proposals still to appear, none of the above approaches to Scripture present themselves as standing convincingly within the Anglican tradition. Doctrine must submit to Scripture. The Archbishop of Canterbury was plain on this point in his 2007 Advent letter. We stand under Scripture as the rule and ultimate standard of faith and though complex in its development, doctrine rises from Scripture:

> Our obedience to the call of Christ the Word Incarnate is drawn
> out first and foremost by our listening to the Bible and conforming
> our lives to what God both offers and requires of us through the
> words and narratives of the Bible. We recognise each other in one
> fellowship when we see one another "standing under" the word of

Scripture. Because of this recognition, we are able to consult and reflect together on the interpretation of Scripture and to learn in that process. Understanding the Bible is not a private process or something to be undertaken in isolation by one part of the family. Radical change in the way we read cannot be determined by one group or tradition alone.[13]

Thus, proponents of same-sex blessings/marriage offer neither a coherent doctrinal statement about same-sex relationships nor a coherent means of testing that statement by "Scripture's witness."

Perhaps, indeed, the treatment of Scripture and doctrine in this debate points to a deeper underlying problem, a generalized loss of confidence among Canadian clergy and people in our Scriptures and the teachings that arise from them. There are deep currents running here, touching on a deep morass in which the church finds itself with regard to the church's Scriptures and their use. Elizabeth Achtemeier describes the situation in the Presbyterian Church:

> Over the last decade, I have been involved through my speaking and writing in the debate that is going on in the church over three pressing issues—the issue of sexuality and homosexuality, the issue of feminism, and the issue of abortion. But the frustration that one experiences in trying to carry on that debate apart from any common recognition of a canon for the church is sometimes overwhelming. For example, what does the church have to say to a woman who claims, "My body is my own," if the church does not know from its canon that we are not our own, but bought with a price and adopted in our baptisms as God's sons and daughters? Or what can the church say to the feminist discussion about the nature of God if it does not hear from its canon that God is not identical with the vital forces of nature, but rather is holy God, totally other than all he has made? Or what can the church say about sexual morality, unless it knows itself from its Scripture to be a covenant people, redeemed from the law, and yet given commandments to guide it in its new life in Christ? The mainline churches are in chaos over these issues, but the debates will never be settled until the church once more confesses that it has a canon, through which there speaks to us the voice of the Triune God.[14]

In this challenging time, the questions posed to the Primate's commission can be seen as an encouraging sign. They seek to take Scripture seriously and to examine the nature of doctrine, and of the development of doctrine. In order for the church's deliberations to be useful in regard to same-sex blessings, however, proponents need to provide a clear proposal for what they are advocating, a definition of same-sex blessings in relation to doctrine and with a specific, concrete and positive scriptural rational, a proposal open to public scrutiny and hardy enough to meld into, or turn over, the catholic faith of the church. Then let the study begin.

NOTES

1. www.skdiocese.com/bishops-writings/2007/7/5/the-bishop-of-sas-katchewans-summer-letter-to-his-clergy-july.html

2. The ecclesiastical trial of Bishop William Righter on heresy charges for his ordination of a practising gay man.

3. Philip Turner, "Episcopal Authority within a Communion of Churches," in *The Fate of Communion: The Agony of Anglicanism and the Future of a Global Church* (Eerdmans, 2006), 135–164, here 147.

4. *The Windsor Report*, 2004 para. 87–96.

5. Stephen Andrews, "Core doctrine and Adiaphora: What's the difference?" Online: http://www.storiesoffaith.ca/inplenary/2007/02/core_doc-trine_and_adiaphora_wh.html

6. *True Union in the Body? A Contribution to the discussion within the Anglican Communion concerning the public blessing of same-sex unions* (2nd ed.; Groves Books, 2003) 11–31.

7. *True Union* 3.26.

8. Walter Wink in an exchange with Robert Gagnon in the *Christian Century*, quoted in *True Union*, n. 35.

9. Elizabeth Achtemeier, "The Canon as the Voice of the Living God," in *Reclaiming the Bible for the Church* (ed. Carl E. Braaten and Robert W. Jenson; Grand Rapids: Eerdmans, 1995), 119–130, here 120.

10. *True Union*, 9–10.

11. These two are contradictory, but that has been overlooked by some advocates who see the advance of "same-sex blessings" as a first step toward

"same-sex marriage."

12. Proposed under the title of "queer theology." See Elizabeth Stuart, *Just Good Friends: Towards a Lesbian and Gay Theology of Relationships* (London: Mowbray, 1995); "Is Lesbian or Gay Marriage an Oxymoron?" in *Celebrating Christian Marriage* (ed. Adrian Thatcher; Edinburg, T&T Clark, 2001), 255–83; *Gay and Lesbian Theologies: Repetitions with Critical Difference* (Aldershot, England: Ashgate, 2003).

13. Rowan Williams, Archbishop's Advent Letter. Online: http://www.anglicancommunion.org/acns/news.cfm/2007/12/14/ACNS4354

14. Elizabeth Achtemeier, *The Canon as the Voice of the Living God*, 120–21.

CHAPTER ELEVEN

A Little Lower Than God

The Integrity and Dignity of Human Persons and Relationships

Peter M. B. Robinson

The appeal to the "integrity" of the human person builds on an understanding of integrity as a quality innate or inherent to the human person. To affirm the integrity of a person and his/her relationship is to affirm their innate goodness, even moral soundness. The biblical understanding of integrity, however, is quite different. It is not simply about the moral soundness or completeness of an individual, nor is it about the moral soundness or completeness of a relationship between two individuals. The word integrity in the biblical text implies wholeness or "holiness" in the sense of how things (people, relations, all of creation) hold together in the context of our relatedness to God. Integrity in the Christian sense of the word has to do with rightly ordered relations with God and the created order, including of course other human beings. The question to be asked, therefore, is what does it mean to affirm the integrity (and by implication the dignity) of human persons and their relationships in the context of a scriptural witness to that integrity?

Certainly the biblical texts challenge us to treat other human beings with dignity and respect. But do we treat them with dignity and respect because of what or who they are in themselves? Or do we treat them with dignity and respect because of who God is and therefore what God has said about them? Furthermore can we, in the context of the scriptural witness, speak about human integrity as a property of an independent autonomous individual or as the property of a relationship between two individuals? These are the questions we want to begin to explore in this paper.

A foundational principle in affirming the dignity and integrity of persons and relations is the doctrine of the *imago Dei*; the affirmation that human beings are made in the image of God. The classic passage for the doctrine of the *imago Dei*, Gen 1:26, 27, speaks of the extraordinary dignity which God confers upon human beings:

> Let us make humankind in our image, according to our likeness; and let them have dominion over the fish of the sea, and over the birds of the air . . . and over every creeping thing that creeps upon the earth.

These words are echoed in Psalm 8. The psalmist says,

> you have made them a little lower than God, and crowned them with glory and honor. You have given them dominion over the works of your hands; you have put all things under their feet (vs. 5, 6 NRSV).

This is a cogent statement of the value that God has placed on human beings. We are a little lower than God. Indeed, we are made in the image of God. These are extraordinary affirmations which seem, in declaring the dignity and worth of human beings, to single humanity out from the rest of creation.

There is a lot that is amazing about human beings: the way we can move, our creative abilities, the way we are able to harness natural forces, our capacity for love. Human beings are extraordinary. There appear to be many reasons why God might have seen and chosen to acknowledge the inherent dignity of humanity.

In spite of the very few scriptural references to the *imago Dei* and the fact that these references remain vague as to the content of the image, the doctrine has played a huge role in human self-understanding. Edward Craig explores the extraordinary influence of the *imago Dei* on philosophical thought in his book *The Mind of God and the Works of Men*. In both theology and philosophy the *imago Dei* has been one of the most significant ideas used to shape our understanding of what it means to "be" human. The influence of this idea has not necessarily corresponded with our understanding of God's formative and sustaining relationship to humanity. Indeed in many cases "god" has become incidental to the discussion. In philosophy, and often in theology as well, the emphasis upon God and what this says about God and how God works in the world has been lost. Instead the focus has been upon what this idea might say or affirm about humanity independent of God.

Indeed the doctrine or the idea that we are made in the image of God has been a jumping-off point for all kinds of speculation about human beings and in particular about the ontological basis of humanity. Being made in the image of God has been seen as a license to devote ourselves to exploring what makes us "god-like." And most of this speculation has centered on human characteristics, on who we are: does being in the image of God mean that we look like God, does it mean that we have a divine spark within us, is it about our intelligence, our freedom, our creativity, or is it simply about how amazing we are?

It is not surprising, given the central role which the *imago Dei* has been given in human self-understanding that in discussions concerning the dignity and integrity of human beings or in the efforts to affirm the rights of the individual, the doctrine of the *imago Dei* has played a central role. In the current debates the *imago Dei* is often cited as a scriptural principle by which we must without question affirm the dignity and integrity of individuals as they are in themselves or as they understand themselves to be. Indeed integrity has come to mean that a person is "being true to themselves." Yet, that is clearly not the point of the doctrine but rather is a direct reversal of the doctrine. The scriptural references to the *imago Dei* are not primarily an affirmation of human capabilities nor do they suggest that human beings possess an "inherent" dignity in and of themselves. Rather, they establish a dignity for human beings rooted not in ourselves or our capabilities but in God and what God has said about us and done for us. However, it is clear that the point of reference for the doctrine has shifted from God to our limited and fallen self-perception. The end result is that we make god in our own image using the *imago Dei* as a way to affirm the person that we perceive ourselves to be.

Being made in the image of God says far more about God than it does about humanity. The affirmation of the dignity of human beings is an affirmation that is primarily rooted not in what we are in ourselves but in God and the love that God has for us. It is a statement about God and his gracious benevolence. The *imago Dei* and the implication of dignity which goes with it is not something intrinsic to human beings but something which is entrusted to human beings by God. That our dignity and integrity is grounded in God rather than ourselves is made particularly clear in Psalm 8. Before declaring the glory and honor that has been conferred on human beings the psalmist asks, "What are human beings that you are mindful of them?" The psalmist expresses amazement that God should place such a high value on human beings. We need to be amazed, to react with wonder, sheer jaw-dropping wonder to the fact that God has asked us to be his representatives and the instruments for his work in the world: you want me, you want us? To be made in the image of God is not primarily a commentary on how amazing we are but how creative and purposeful God is.

Of course being made in the image of God does indeed say something about who we are. The question is whether that "something" exists or can be understood independently of our relatedness to God. If, as has often been assumed, human beings are completely independent and autonomous beings then the *imago Dei* could possibly be identified with something about human beings in their autonomy. If, however, we accept that human beings do not exist in radical autonomy and independence then we cannot understand the *imago Dei* except in terms of human relatedness. In particular we cannot understand what it means to be human, let alone the *imago Dei*, apart from our relatedness to God; Father, Son and Holy Spirit, and our participation (or lack of participation) in his intentions for us. That leads us to consider briefly the way in which humanity is related to the rest of creation.

The place of humanity in relationship to the rest of creation is clearly established in both Genesis and Psalm 8. Speaking of humanity the psalmist says *"You have given them dominion over the works of your hands; you have put all things under their feet."* Old Testament scholars tell us that at the heart of the image is our call to exercise dominion or stewardship. Whether we understand stewardship as integral to the image or a natural consequence of the image it is clear that humanity has been entrusted with a sacred responsibility. God has chosen human beings for an extraordinary and daunting task: to be his representatives and to exercise his rule over all living things. The image of God either by implication or by definition involves a right ordering in relationship with God and with the created realm.

That brings us to speak more directly about the "integrity" of human beings and their relations or relationships. When we speak of the integrity of human beings or of human relationships we cannot speak of that in isolation from the rest of the created order nor indeed in isolation from the context of our relationship to God. God's identification of human beings is not an identification which singles humanity out but clearly identifies them in the context of their relatedness first to God himself and secondly to the rest of creation.[1]

Instead, the assumption has been that to be in the image of God says something about humanity, something that makes us special or distinct from the rest of the created order; seeing ourselves as a little lower than God has meant, or so it has been assumed, that humanity is superior to everything else on the face of the earth. Much of the inquiry into what it means to be made in the image of God and therefore what it means to be human has been sought through a process of comparison and contrast with the rest of the created order. In other words the ontological question of what a human being "is" has been answered through the comparative question which is "what is it about human beings that makes them special or unique in contrast to the rest of the created order?" (This is a point made by Colin Gunton in *Persons Divine and Human*).

The end result of this speculative approach has been a tendency to look for an element or characteristic of human beings which differentiates humans from the rest of creation. That element has then been identified as the ontological or central basis of what it means to be human. Historically the most common answer to the ontological question has been human rationality: it is our rational capacity which not only distinguishes us from the rest of creation but is also that element which is most "godlike" about us. This approach to understanding what it means to be human lies at the root of the physical/spiritual dualism which is such an integral and destructive aspect of Western thought. In one stroke we have identified human rationality as the basis of what it means to be truly human as well as laying the foundation for the modern notion of a person as an independent and autonomous being. Inevitably, this has also led to the tendency to try to understand human beings in isolation from their relationship to the rest of creation and their relationship to God. (This has significant implications for a Christian attitude or response to the environmental movement but that is far outside the scope of this short paper). In other words the way in which the *imago Dei* has been understood has led us to consider human beings as they are in themselves, independent of the matrix of relations to the physical world and to God.

The result is twofold. First, as has already been mentioned, there is the idea of humans as independent and autonomous beings, i.e. as individuals. This in turn has meant that when we talk about affirming the dignity or integrity of a person we look at who they are in themselves or we look to affirm their individual existence. One result of this perspective is that human beings have continued to live in ways that have hindered or even blocked God's rule and God's glory rather than enabling God's rule in the world. For example we interpreted dominion as the right to domination, the right to do what we want to do. Since we thought we were superior to the animals and the plants we also thought we could treat them however we wanted to treat them. We have exercised our power in the world in a way that has denied God's goodness and purpose instead of fulfilling them. Or to put that another way, rather than acting and living in the image of God human beings have done exactly the opposite. We have denied God, we have denied his image, and we have denied the truth of who we are. We have been in danger of destroying the very gift that God has given to us and in danger of destroying ourselves in the process. In our rebellion we have squandered God's resources; we have lost sight of what we are to do.

WHAT HAPPENED:

What is so clear in both Gen 1:26–27 and Psalm 8 is that the focus is on God—what he has done in us and for us and what he is asking us to do for him as his representatives. God made us in his image so that we would have the necessary resources to do the job that he has asked us to do. Our position over all things is sheer gift. In a right relationship with God and in right relationships with other human beings and with the rest of the created order we are to help hold the world together. The worst possible thing is that we begin to think it is our privilege, our right or our due; or that it says something about who we are in ourselves. Yet that is exactly what we have done. We have focused on what these passages say about us rather than what they say about God. And here is where it all began to fall apart. Human beings have been so busy trying to figure out what being in the Image said about *us* that we have taken our eyes off God and his desires for us and focused instead on how special we are. As a result not only have we confused what it means to be in the image of God but we have also damaged or marred that image.

RENEWAL: THE IMAGE IN THE NEW TESTAMENT

When the Image is spoken of in the New Testament it refers primarily to Jesus Christ. When it speaks of human beings it does not confirm the image as a natural property of our humanity. Instead it suggests that the image is something we see in Christ to which we must be conformed. *"For those whom he foreknew he also predestined to be conformed to the image of his Son, in order that he might be the first-born within a large family"* (Rom 8:29 NRSV). Whereas Genesis tells us that we were made in the image of God, Romans tells us that we are to be conformed to the image of his Son. That suggests several things. First, it suggests that the image has been affected in a significant way by the Fall, by human rebellion against God. Second, the image is not a "natural" property of humanity but is something clearly rooted in God. Third, the image and the realization of the image cannot be understood apart from the context of our relatedness to God. Fourth, conformity to the image demands transformation. This means that the image remains an eschatological goal rather than a fully present reality. The nature of a human person cannot be understood or realized without reference to the finality of all things.

In Jesus Christ we not only see God clearly, we also see the original and intended shape for humanity. We see the way in which human beings were intended to "hold all things together" as well as being held together. In other words we see the basis for integrity in a Christian perspective. To be conformed to Jesus is to become fully human, to move from being a distorted humanity in rebellion against God to being true humanity in relationship with God. To be conformed to the image of God then means allowing God to challenge us to the very core of our being, to challenge absolutely everything about us.

The *imago Dei* is not therefore a statement which points toward the inherent dignity or integrity of human beings. Rather it is a dignity that is accorded to human beings because of who God is and an integrity that is realized as we find our coherence or wholeness in a right relationship to God in Christ and in right relationships to the rest of creation. Likewise, the affirmation of the dignity or integrity of human beings does not lead to a blanket affirmation of the goodness and worth of the individual. Nor can it be used to affirm certain aspects, characteristics or orientations of our humanity regardless of how fundamental we believe those aspects might be.

Integrity in a Christian context must refer not simply to moral uprightness but to the way in which things (people and creation) hold together, and particularly the way in which we and our relationships are rightly ordered in relationship with God. Integrity must be understood not in individual terms but ecclesially—and this not simply in terms of people "getting along" with one another or "putting up" with one another, but in allowing our lives and relationships to be re-centred and reordered in Jesus Christ. We cannot affirm someone as having acted with integrity or having behaved with integrity simply because they have done what they thought was right, because they have behaved in a way that is true to "who they are." Rather it has to do with learning to live in the reconciliation which has been effected by Christ. Integrity has to do with our being re-centred with new hearts, new desires, and new wills which are rooted in God's desires for us rather than our desires for ourselves.

NOTES

1. Even the notion of relationships which we use in speaking of human beings is rooted in an individualistic notion of our "choosing" the one to whom we want to relate. This is what renowned philosopher Charles Taylor calls the debased notion of the modern love relationship where two individuals "choose" to be in relationship with each other.

BIBLIOGRAPHY

Craig, Edward. *The Mind of God and the Works of Man.* Oxford: Clarendon Press, 1985.

Gunton, Colin. "Trinity, Ontology and Anthropology: Towards a Renewal of the Doctrine of the *Imago Dei.*" Pages 47-64 in *Persons Divine and Human.* Edited by C. Schwoebel and C. Gunton. Edinburgh: T&T Clark, 1991.

Taylor, Charles. *Sources of the Self.* Cambridge: Cambridge University Press, 1989.

CHAPTER TWELVE

"Sanctity" and "Holiness" in the Biblical Theology of Human Relationships

Ian H. Henderson

What is "sanctity" in human relationships and how does sanctity relate to personal, psychological, social and moral integrity? Neither English nor the languages of Scripture and/or Tradition provide rigidly defined, strictly separated vocabulary for "sanctity" and "holiness" and related terms such as "the sacred," "sacrality," "consecration" and "dedication." In some languages the texts of Scripture itself, for example, are "Holy" or "Sainte," while in others they are "Sacra." At most we may say that "sanctity" and especially its more Anglo-Saxon, folksier synonym, "holiness," may suggest on balance a greater sense of moral distinction than does the more abstract, "sacredness." In English translation it can be difficult to appreciate that apparently technical terms such as "priest," "temple," "sacrifice" are biblically integral to this field of meanings. In Greek, for example, "priest," can be *hiereus*, transparently a "holy person"; "temple," *hieron*, is likewise "holy place," and "sacrifices" may be described simply as *hiera*, "sacred things." Often, especially in Protestant cultures nervous about anything that smacks of "ritual," "holiness" has been reduced to a category of moral and spiritual perfection, the end of a process of essentially personal "sanctification." In biblical theology such terms do indeed often express some moral content, but they always resonate with more-than-just-moral aspects of our created relationship with God.

Modern theories of religion have embraced "the holy" (Rudolph Otto [1869–1937]) and "the sacred" (Émile Durkheim [1858–1917]) as potentially universal fields of meaning and human experience. "The holy" or "the sacred" is often taken to transcend or, rather, underlie the plurality of particular religious and moral traditions across humanity. At least since Friedrich Schleiermacher (1768–1834), a central value of the liberal tradition in Christianity has been the cultivation of humanity's presumably innate "sense of absolute dependence" on the divine and holy, however apprehended. On such a view, the "sacred" and the "holy" are at best instrumental to the self-discovery of human nature, while at worst they may be instruments of its oppression. Secular modernity has in consequence often been characterised as the "disenchantment of the world" (Marcel Gauchet), the breaking of ancient spells and emancipation from ancient spiritual, moral and social bondage. For some, such disenchantment is ironically the one remaining sacred mission, the eradication of superstition, fanaticism, and intolerance (Voltaire [1759–1770] «écraser l'Infâme»). For others, especially Anglicans (!), such disenchantment is not absolute, but selective, controlled by autonomous moral and political values.

For many Christians in late modernity, such disenchantment is and ought to be irreversible, even if religion ought to try to mitigate secularity's harshest side-effects. We don't want to ignore the Enlightenment's challenge to religious tradition. Yet we do acknowledge that the experience of modernity as the quest for personal autonomy has also incurred terrible costs of social, cultural-religious and ecological alienation. Such costs might perhaps be usefully tempered by a deliberate re-sacralization of our relationship with each other and with the rest of creation. One fascinating aspect of the "post-modern" is the curious attempt to re-sacralize ourselves, our new relationships and our changing environment *without appeal to God's transcendence as the source of sacrality*, surely in one sense a consequence of Schleiermacher's approach.

On balance, however, the biblical language of holiness, of sacred things and of sacred, covenant relationships works against such a project of the ethically or aesthetically or politically selective re-enchantment of an emancipated humanity and a commodified world. On the one hand, the language of holiness, sacredness, and, hence, of sacrifice and dedication in the Scriptures of Israel and the church retains a robustly, even crudely, material emphasis. It is, above all, places and things, foods, fluids, bodies and buildings that are said to be holy or consecrated. The holiness of human persons and their relationships is therefore not primarily a moral/ethical quality. Rather, holiness is an otherwise arbitrary point of contact between the world and our creator. Even, or especially, the holiness of God is centrally about God's immanence in the material, temporal and human order, an immanence which is rightly experienced as frightening and overpowering, dangerous to handle.

Paul's concrete understanding of sacramental, eucharistic eating in Christianity and in idolatry is perhaps the most accessible illustration of this intensified materiality and relationality of the holy (1 Cor 10–11): meat ritually consecrated as sacrifice to idols has no intrinsic, magical quality to injure those who eat, yet conscious eating of sacrificial meat as such can have grave consequences for relationship with God, others—and even demons. Similarly from the opposite direction, inappropriate eating and drinking of the church's consecrated cup and loaf, without respect for the sheer corporeality and mortality of Christ for us, has consequences which moderns find shockingly corporeal and mortal. Paul's understanding of the sacrality of our eucharistic relationship with Christ (or with idols!) is here puzzling or even offensive to Enlightenment readers, but is entirely consistent with biblical norms of holiness.

On the other hand, the intense materiality of the holy is limited by the sense of separation of the holy/sacred from the rest of the material world. *This* place/person/bodily state/thing is holy/sacred in part because *those other* places/persons/bodily states/things are not. The decisive opposite of "holy" for most purposes is not "accursed" or "evil," but "profane," "ordinary," "commonplace," even "secular." The holy and the sacred only have meaning in the context of God's positive relation to the value of the unhallowed ordinary. That this particular water or bread or wine is to be consecrated for sacred use is thus neither a denigration of all other water or bread or wine nor a denial of those ordinary qualities of water, bread and wine that make them symbolically interesting for elective, occasional ritual hallowing. In terms of the ordinary virtues of food, ordinary food (though still to a degree consecrated by the gratitude of those who receive it as God's gift) is always at least as nutritious as the more sacralized portion set apart for ritual use. The "extra" meaning of the consecrated comes essentially from the act of election and consecration, in deliberate tension with the ancillary, borrowed symbolism of ordinary matter.

Moreover, in ritual performance the opposite of "a blessing" may be "a curse," but both the "blessed" and the "accursed" are essentially opposed to the ordinary. Above all, Jesus Christ, incarnate and crucified, is the ultimate intersection of "curse" and "blessing," the final cause and focus of all meaningful relatedness toward God (Galatians 3). In Jesus and in many of those Jesus touches curse and blessing become complementary opposites differentiating redeemed sinners from the indeterminate mediocrity of an idolatrously self-sufficient world.

For Israel in particular the possession and use of God's specifically separated, consecrated Land requires formal recognition in the further separation and return to God of tithes and first-fruits of agricultural produce; use of time itself requires the consecration of the Sabbath, use even of the body requires the ritual separation of the foreskin, of menstrual blood and other body fluids and the payment to the temple of money for the life of each Israelite male. Hallowing in this way of a token or a part does not imply rejection of the whole, but rather its conditional availability as God's gift to a receptive humanity.

The "holy land" is thus not holy because it is geographically better than other real estate, nor does the Land of Promise belong to Israel by any right of property. Instead both the Land and the People have been set aside, apart from other lands and peoples, by God's election, for God's enjoyment and only therefore for each other: election may indeed prefer to assert itself by preferring the intrinsically unprepossessing. Similarly some foods are kosher for Israel, not because they are an objectively better diet, but because God has made them sacred for Israel. The "Holy Bible" is not a collection of books which are as literature better than other options: Jews and Christians have always had other, beautiful, religious books. Rather the Bible is holy because God's election has given these books to Israel and the church as sacred: the long and decentralized processes of canon-formation are only secondarily processes of literary and theological reflection. Finally, the church itself is holy, not because the "saints," the "holy ones," are morally better people than our neighbours, but because God has gathered and consecrated precisely this community of sinners to be the body and the bride of Christ here and now. So also marriage is uniquely holy in the biblical tradition not because marriage is always better, ethically, than other human relationships (friendship, citizenship, scholarship, kinship, kingship, etc.), but primarily because God has designed and designated it as such.

Even "ritual impurity," the extreme opposite pole from "holiness" and "sanctity," beyond the gracious, God-given ordinariness of the weekday and mundane, is not always the horrible soul-destroying curse which modern moralising Bible-reading often makes it out to be. Most ritual impurity imposes little more than a duty of sacred hygiene—a bath and a delay before entering the temple's sacred space. More serious dimensions of ritual impurity often come not as curse, but as sacred obligation: corpse impurity becomes the last solemn duty for a child honouring a parent. In rabbinic Judaism, the sacred Torah Scroll imparts a degree of ritual impurity on the hands, so that, even when worn out, the physical medium of God's holy law cannot simply be thrown out or recycled. The sanctity and sacredness of selected human relationships and of selected aspects (for example, sexual) of certain human relationships do not therefore (and should not) always automatically entail the rejection and marginalization either of the ordinary or of the impure, as indeed Jesus tried to show.

The sanctity/holiness/sacredness of a human relationship is thus not constituted in the relationship itself as the product of its participants' moral agency alone. Rather sanctity of things, bodies, persons, and their relationships arises from the presence and holiness of God distilling itself through the whole sacred identity of Israel and the church as God's covenant people. The essential condition of holiness in human relationships is thus God's election, separating Israel and the church as priestly communities within humanity. It is painfully clear that God's election of Jews and Christians into emphatically special relationship does not confer moral superiority over the rest of humanity. But the holy "covenant" relationship does place select human relationships in a context of relative holiness.

More often, more emphatically, and more consistently than any other relationship, the marriage relation is biblically represented as primordial and prior to the covenant separating Israel and the church within humanity. Marriage is the separation and special consecration to one another of Adam and Eve within the rest of the created order. Adam and Eve are separated from the rest of creation and dedicated by God to each other not in order to marginalize other possibilities for human (and natural) relationship, but as the pre-condition for naming such other possibilities. Marriage is indeed peculiarly available as an analogue to the covenant relation between God/Christ and Israel/the Church, because marriage holiness and its practical outcome, "righteousness," occur only inside the special relationship of a covenant community (ideally a covenant with God), which is never merely a voluntary association. "After the Fall" marriage remains prophetically available as a privileged standpoint from which to evaluate other human relationships, including actual marriages and relatively marital relationships between sinners.

One positive value in the reconsideration of marriage in the context of late modern perceptions of sexuality is that marriage is an ideal test case for abandoning the failed and unbiblical distinction between a "moral law" and a "ceremonial law": the marriage relationship has both moral and ceremonial qualities, but its holiness does not reside in either, but in God's election of marriage as preferred analogy to Christ's relationship with the church (Ephesians 5). Scripture does not sustain any systematic distinction between "moral law(s)" and "ceremonial law(s)": such a distinction has too long distorted Christianity toward an antinomian moralism that divides the Torah according to our perceptions of value ("moral" is good and permanent; "ceremonial" is at best contingent, if not always bad). (Moral and ceremonial law is, moreover, inseparable from doctrinal law as in Israel's confession of the oneness of God.) Scripture does, however, support other distinctions within Torah: between duties arising from our love of God and duties arising from our love of neighbour; between law defining the covenant distinctiveness of Israel/the Church and law which moderates the human condition universally; perhaps most beautifully, between the Torah of the hand-made temple and the Torah of the virgin-born Incarnation (Matt 12:6; John 1). The availability in the Torah of the marriage covenant to serve as privileged analogy of the covenant between God and Israel/Christ and the church arises in part from the fact that marriage is clearly not confined to Israel or to the church: it is in itself and in each instantiation a "great mystery," available to be referred to the complementary mystery of ecclesial existence. Indeed, even morally disastrous marriage can become a prophetic sign of the sin-damaged covenant (Hosea).

The most important change during the last century in scholarly understanding of Scripture and of Jesus himself has been the recognition, post-Christendom and post-Holocaust, that Jesus remains forever a Jew. Jesus is a Jew not only in some accidental cultural-ethnic sense, but also programmatically and eschatologically. Historical Jesus research and New Testament exegesis have often been used to provide ammunition for the cultural battles of our day. An overwhelmingly positive result of such study, however, has been the realisation that neither Jesus nor Paul understood the gospel to be a religious system in opposition to Judaism as a religious system. Many implications of this recognition for restoring Jewish-Christian relationships have been drawn in the church, but the implications for Christian self-understanding have met greater resistance. Christians who have begun to value Judaism, nevertheless, often remain committed to a view of Torah-observance as obviated by the work of Christ. Against such a view, the critical difference between (non-Christian) Judaism and Christianity is Christological. "[W]hat is wrong with the law is that it is not Christ" (E. P. Sanders 1977, 551). Consequently, only defective Christologies, of Jesus as little more than a moral example and teacher, need (falsely) to accuse Judaism (or Catholicism or Puritanism . . .) of "legalism," of claiming that the law validates the covenant relationship. Overwhelmingly, both Jewish and Christian normative texts recognize that Torah-observance has meaning only inside the sanctity of the covenant relationship freely given by God. Both Judaism and Christianity intend to practise "covenantal nomism" (E. P. Sanders). If some human identities and relationships are "holy," then, it is not because of their moral success or integrity (valuable in itself), but because of their prior election.

Thus Jesus kept kosher, observed Sabbath, ate Passover and in his resurrection bears on his body not only the marks of the cross, but also presumably that of his circumcision. In Christian history, Jesus has all too often been read and preached as a rebel against Jewish legalism and Pharisaic authority—with tragic consequences in antinomian and anti-Jewish reception. No action attributed to Jesus in Scripture constitutes a violation of Torah; many of Jesus' words and deeds surely challenge Israelite holiness and transform its horizons, but Jesus' challenge is from within the special election of the holiness covenant. It is Jesus' chosen Twelve who one day will judge a renewed Israel while the Son of Man judges the world and its kingdoms (Matt 19:28).

Two little case studies may usefully show Scripture reasoning about inter-human relationship through categories of sanctity/holiness. Mark 7 brings together several traditions of Jesus criticising the Pharisaic use of "tradition" to trump written Torah. The author of Mark's Gospel seems centrally interested in such material in order to support the inference (Mark 7:19) that Jesus would not extend kosher-observance to Mark's non-Jewish readers (not the same thing, by the way, as abolishing *kashrut* outright). There are, however, easier ways to argue that non-Jews don't need to keep kosher. Mark's Jesus is doing something more complex than merely emancipating his (gentile) followers from Jewish food norms. I think he is diminishing the normative distance between the love of God (*qorban* and *kashrut*) and love of neighbour (honouring parents).

Jesus, therefore, in an unusually specific example, gives his nearest approach to an explicit treatment of the abstraction "holiness." Before saying anything about eating and food, Jesus attacks the strategy of dedicating one's belongings to God or to God's temple as "*qorban*" as a way of avoiding having to use one's property to support father or mother. Jesus is interested in the intentions of someone who might set up such a "holy trust" for his property, but Jesus is also taking seriously the more objective problem of whether voluntarily taking on an obligation to God takes precedence over accepting the compulsory obligation to my father and mother laid on me by God's law. If (cynically or sincerely) I have dedicated my property to God, can I take some of it to take care of my parents instead? Jesus doesn't actually adjudicate on the property question, instead he characteristically insists on the sacred demand of parent-child relationship under Torah (for Jews and non-Jews alike). Here as elsewhere in Jesus' Torah-teaching the love of neighbour is a remarkably close second to the love of God. Further, Jesus insists that special religious expertise is not the solution to the reader's problem of ranking Torah obligations. The sacredness of selected human relationships under the second table of the law (love of neighbour) is indeed secondary to the sacredness of the relationship with God under the first table (love of God). But Jesus warns emphatically against using the one to avoid the other. Whatever I do with my property (or my food), I must find the means to honour my father and my mother within a human relationship which is almost as sacred as the relationship with God/the temple itself.

Similarly alien to modern notions of moral holiness, yet consistent with the concrete mentality of Scripture, are Paul's comments on the "holiness" of an unbelieving husband or wife and of the children of a Christian and a non-Christian (I Cor 7:12–16). Paul's discussion of the sanctity of the marriage relationship even between a believer and an unbeliever is in every way remarkable. The unbelieving partner is "made holy" by the fact of being married, both sexually and socially united, with a believer. Inside the marriage covenant, the holiness of the believing partner in some sense generally overrides the non-purity of a partner who, after all, is in most of the cases Paul has in mind not merely non-believing, but actively participant in the idolatrous cultic and sexual life of the mainstream of Corinthian society.

Paul's high valuation of the sanctity of the marriage covenant is here manifestly not confined to marriages between Christians and/or between observant Jews, but extends in principle or potentially even to marriages between idolaters (one of whom subsequently becomes a Christian)! Moreover, on the one hand, Paul is thinking of relational holiness, of the sanctity of human relationships, in the deeply concrete, biblical terms of bodily and social contamination; sexual intimacy in marriage is the vector along which "sanctity" is transmitted just as sexual intimacy in other contexts is the vector of ritual contamination of "the temple" (6:12–20).

On the other hand, surprisingly, it is the contagious sanctity of the believer which determines the ritual character of the mixed relationship. This must reflect the bias of marriage toward transmitting holiness rather than impurity; within the system constituted by the marriage relationship there is greater conductivity for the positive holiness of the believing partner than for the negative charge of the unbelieving spouse. Ephesians 5 is the *locus classicus* for the holiness of marriage as such; Paul's discussion in 1 Corinthians is rather about the holiness of the individual Christian and its transmissibility and/or corruptibility in sexual and cultic relationships. From an understandable covenantal, perhaps Jewish, point of view, in a mixed marriage the holiness of the believing partner and of the relationship itself might well be ritually compromised by the continually reinforced ritual impurity of a non-observant spouse; from a certain societal, perhaps Greco-Roman, point of view, it might be thought that the initiation of two spouses into different mysteries would (except around major festivals . . .) be ritually neutral as regards the sanctity of the marriage itself. Yet for Paul, the sanctity of a body/person in touch with Jesus Christ is, within the intimacy of the marriage bond, positively communicable to a spouse and to children. Indeed, again astonishingly, Paul adduces the sanctity of the children of a mixed marriage as evidence for (not as a further inference from) the holiness of the unbelieving spouse in a mixed marriage (1 Cor 7:14). The main implication of the imputed sanctity of the unbelieving partner is perhaps to make the marriage indissoluble by the Christian partner. All this notwithstanding Paul still makes unusually flexible (indeed, notoriously unclear) concessions to the likelihood of breakdown in such mixed marriages: if the unbeliever leaves, the believer is not bound (1 Cor 7:15).

What is clear here is that the sanctity of these human relationships does not rest upon or indicate their moral or eschatological status. Paul's criterion here is not the moral acceptability of the relationships or the persons involved: Paul is not expressing admiration for the relationships in question and is certainly not recommending that believers and non-believers routinely marry. Clearly, again, "sanctity of relationship" does not by any means correspond simply with moral integrity or ecclesial acceptability: the Christian's spouse and children, though made "holy" to the church because of the marriage covenant, do not become honorary Christians. Thus specifically, Paul is able to hope that the Christian spouse may prove instrumental to the eventual salvation of the still non-Christian, yet already holy, spouse (v. 16).

Sanctity is biblically a characteristic only of select phenomena and, hence, of select human relationships which have a liminal, threshold function between God and the world. This must be clearly distinguished from the modern tendency to affirm relational sanctity based on perceived moral virtues. Attributing sanctity to a human relationship is profoundly different than recognizing in it the moral virtue of integrity. Biblically the exceptional sanctity of the marriage relationship arises from its election as the privileged analogue for the covenant between God/Christ and Israel/the Church. Still, it is the intense ritual conductivity of sexual intimacy in (or outside of) marriage which makes sexual relationship a peculiarly powerful vocabulary for enacting the "great mystery."

In Jesus' distillation of biblical covenant history, perhaps the "kingship" or "sovereignty of God" is the only comparable privileging of a human relational analogue to God's action in the world: among human relationships, only the State (with all its tragic failings) has anything like as good a claim, biblically, as marriage and the *ekklesia* to be a sacred institution.

REFERENCES:

Émile Durkheim [1858–1917]. *The Elementary Forms of Religious Life.* Translated by Carol Cosman; abridged with an introduction and notes by Mark S. Cladis. Oxford/New York: Oxford University Press, 2001. Originally published as: *Les formes élémentaires de la vie religieuse: le système totémique en Australie.* (1912)

Marcel Gauchet. *The Disenchantment of the World: A Political History of Religion.* Translated by Oscar Burge; with a foreword by Charles Taylor. Princeton, N.J.: Princeton University Press, 1997. Originally published as: *Désenchantement du monde: une histoire politique de la religion.* (1985)

Rudolph Otto [1869–1937]. *The Idea of the Holy: An Inquiry into the Non-rational Factor in the Idea of the Divine and its Relation to the Rational.* Translated by John W. Harvey. Second ed. New York: Oxford University Press, 1950. Originally published as: *Das Heilige: über das Irrationale in der Idee des Göttlichen und sein Verhältnis zum Rationalen.* (1917)

E. P. Sanders. *Paul and Palestinian Judaism.* London: SCM, 1977. This is the book that inaugurated the new perspective on Paul and, hence, on Judaism.

E. P. Sanders. *Paul, the Law, and the Jewish People.* Philadelphia: Fortress Press, 1983. This is a relatively accessible presentation of Sanders' landmark study of Paul.

E. P. Sanders. *Jesus and Judaism.* Philadelphia: Fortress Press, 1985. This is a somewhat more technical study of similar issues in the context of historical Jesus research.

Friedrich Schleiermacher (1768–1834). *The Christian Faith* (Edinburgh: T. & T. Clark, 1928); originally published as: *Der christliche Glaube nach den Grundsätzen der evangelischen Kirche im Zusammenhange dargestellt.* (1821/22)

CHAPTER THIRTEEN

Sex and the Garden:

Genesis 3 and the Sanctity of Human Relationships

Catherine Sider Hamilton

The Primate's questions raise one of the central claims of the argument for same-sex blessings: namely, that human relationships, in this case specifically same-sex relationships, have "sanctity." Behind the question of "Scripture's witness to the integrity of every human person and the question of the sanctity of human relationships" lies the motion passed by General Synod 2004: that this Synod "affirm the sanctity and integrity of committed same-sex relationships." This appears to be a bald affirmation of the innate or natural holiness of same-sex relationships. Indeed, the argument for same-sex blessings has proceeded in part on the basis of an argument from nature arising from a reading of Genesis 1. Nature is God's creation; nature includes the human being; what God created God declared "very good"; we are therefore, in our natural state, good. Our sexual drives are part of this natural state; they are therefore good. Hence the language of blessing: to bless same-sex relationships is to recognize their inherent blessedness. It is also to bless God—to recognize that the creator God has blessed us in this aspect of our created lives, and to thank God for the blessing. The sanctity of the sexual relationship follows from the sanctity of the person as a sexual being. A rite of same-sex blessing (which is indistinguishable from marriage, insofar as the only priestly act in a marriage is the blessing) is therefore theologically appropriate: it recognizes the natural sanctity of the relationship itself.

The argument for the sanctity of same-sex relationships has a certain immediate appeal: every sunset, every newborn child is a reminder that God's creation is full of goodness and beauty; why not, then, our sexual drives too? The question asked by the Primate and General Synod 2007, however, is how the claim to natural sanctity stands up against "Scripture's witness." I propose to consider the claim against a close reading of Genesis 3 and against two early scriptural interpretations of Genesis 3, in Susanna and in Paul. I suggest we will find that both a close reading of the story of the serpent in the garden, and the history of its interpretation, do not in fact uphold either the claim to innate holiness for sexual relationships or the theology underlying that claim. Rather, they tell a story of a good creation gone awry and God's work in Christ to redeem it, a story that issues for us in the mysterious joy of a cross-shaped life.

The claim to natural sanctity meets an immediate obstacle in Genesis 3. There seems to be no place, in the paean to the goodness of God's creation reflected in our natural lives, for the problem of sin. What happens to the people whom God created good (in his image) when they turn away from God? Interestingly, the Jewish and early Christian reading of Genesis 3 saw the immediate consequence of Adam and Eve's disobedience to God in two things: the loss of the closer walk with God (in the garden at the time of the evening breeze) and the loss of sexual innocence. And these two things are related. "The man and his wife were both naked, and were not ashamed" (Gen 2:25): that is the summary comment the creation narrative in Genesis 2 makes about the life of Adam and Eve in the garden before the entrance of the serpent. The Hebrew verb "to be ashamed" (here in the *hithpael*) indicates shame "before one another" (BDB)—sexual innocence, that is, serves to sum up the uncorrupted state of the human being, what it means to be in a state of natural goodness. Conversely, it is the loss of sexual innocence in particular, and a concomitant awakening of shame, that marks their disobedience. When Eve takes the fruit and gives it to her husband and they both eat, "the eyes of both were opened, and they knew that they were naked" (Gen 3:7); therefore they hide from God (Gen 3:8, 10).

The text of Genesis itself thus links the disruption of the original human relationship to God precisely to the disruption of the human sexual relationship. Later biblical interpreters of this text read it in just this way, building from it a theology of human separation from God and from self, evidenced in corrupted sexual desire. Sexual desire (*epithumia*), far from enacting the natural goodness of the human being, reveals the corruption and anguish of the human heart.

Two texts, one a Jewish narrative from the second century B.C.E., the other Paul's letter to the Romans, illustrate this reading. The story of Susanna retells (as George Brooke shows)[1] the story of Eve in the garden in order, through the righteous Susanna, to reverse it. It is a story of human sin vs. human obedience to God, and it centres in sexual desire. It is because of desire (*epithumia*) that the lascivious elders hide in the garden and watch Susanna. They try to force sex upon her; when she refuses they try to force her death. Her obedience to God in refusing adultery, her innocence and her turning to God in the face of death form a deliberate contrast to Adam and Eve in that other garden—their disobedience, their loss of innocence, their consequent hiding from God. Susanna's prayer saves her, through Daniel and by the grace of God: life, not death, is the outcome of her story, in contrast to the story of Adam and Eve. In this way the Jewish author of Susanna reverses the story of Eve: the righteous and beautiful woman chooses obedience to God in the garden, and finds that it is for her the way of life. What is crucial for our purposes is that the problem in Susanna's garden is sexual sin: *epithumia*, lust. The elders' *epithumia* sums up their corruption (their "wickedness," as the text puts it): their history not only of sexual abuse (Sus 57), but of hypocrisy and injustice, though they are judges of Israel. And it is Susanna's sexual purity that enacts her righteousness and turns shame into innocence (Sus 63) and death into life (Sus 62). This narrator reads the story of Genesis as linking the problem of sin in general to the problem of sexual sin. What happened when Adam and Eve turned away from God in the garden? *Epithumia*, of which disordered sexual desire is paradigmatic, was born.

So, too, for Paul. When in Romans 7 Paul describes the anguished lot of the person sold under sin, he calls up the story of Eden ("sin, *taking opportunity* through the *commandment, deceived* me, and through it *killed* me" [Rom 7:11]—in Genesis 3 the serpent takes opportunity through what God commanded [Gen 3:11, 17] to "deceive" Eve [Gen 3:13], thereby bringing death upon her). What is the sin that is for Paul paradigmatic? It is *epithumia*: "but sin taking opportunity through the commandment worked in me *'pasan epithumian,'* every kind of desire." Paul, like Susanna, reading the problem of human sin through Genesis 3, sees it as centred in *epithumia*. Against the background of Genesis 3's emphasis on the loss of sexual innocence, against the background of Susanna's reading of Genesis 3 in terms of sexual sin, the word *epithumia* in Paul's retelling of Genesis 3 evokes exactly the same problem. "Every kind of desire" emphatically includes, in this context, sexual desire. The commandment against coveting (*ouk epithumeseis*) itself further underscores the meaning of sexual desire inherent in *epithumia*: it reads in part (and, in Deuteronomy, with emphasis): You shall not covet your neighbour's wife (Exod 20:17; Deut 5:21). So Paul, like Susanna, reads the problem of sin created by Adam and Eve's disobedience in Genesis 3 as, paradigmatically, a problem of *epithumia*: desire, especially sexual desire.

These two works may stand as representative of a tradition of interpretation spanning centuries and historical settings, a tradition, moreover, which has in Paul found a place in the canon of Scripture. This tradition reads Genesis 3 as a story of the distortion of human nature and of the human relationship to God. Susanna's elders, however they were created, are no longer good; Paul's "ego" is torn in two between the desires of the flesh and the will of the mind for good. The human person is no longer free simply to be "good": the loss of the intimate walk with God entails also the loss of innocence. And the loss of sexual innocence, of a sexual life untroubled by distorted desires, serves to symbolize the larger human problem. The declaration of the inherent goodness of the human person and human sexual relationships thus runs exactly counter to the biblical story, as it is told in Genesis and retold in later biblical witnesses. This is one significant problem with General Synod's affirmation.

A second problem follows from the first. The argument for same-sex blessing, as it is reflected in the decisions of our General Synod, moves from the inherent "sanctity" of same-sex relationships to the legitimacy of blessing them. But this is contrary to the logic of Scripture. In the whole span of Scripture, human relationships are "good" for exactly one verse. From then on, from Genesis 3 to Revelation, the scriptural story moves from the corruption of the relationship between Adam and Eve to its redemption. The logic of blessedness, that is, moves from the redeeming act of God to the consequent holiness of the relationship. It is important to note that the New Testament does not impute "goodness" to the human person. Indeed, Jesus in Mark's gospel emphatically denies that people can be called "good." "Why do you call me 'good'?" he says. "No one is good but God alone" (Mark 10:18). Instead, the New Testament talks about "sanctification" or "holiness." If humans are created good at the beginning of the biblical story, at the end of the story, in the New Testament, they are *made* good: they are sanctified. Sanctity is not a natural property; it is a gift of God.

Paul describes sanctity as the cleansing of the human person and the putting right of the human relationship with God: "but you were washed, you were sanctified ("made holy," *hagiao*), you were justified in the name of the Lord Jesus Christ and by the Spirit of our God" (1 Cor 6:11). Sanctity requires washing because people are enmeshed in all sorts of corrupt and corrupting behaviour: they are *"pornoi"* ("fornicators," to use the crusty old translation), idol-worshippers, adulterers, involved in male-to-male sex, thieves, drunks, loud-mouthed and abusive (1 Cor 6:9–10.) So were some of you, Paul says—but no longer, because you have been baptized into Christ. Sanctity comes through Christ, in the Spirit. It is made accessible to us by the work of Christ, by his death for our sins (Rom 5:8 *et passim*), the saving death into which we are baptized. And by this baptism we are changed. No longer slaves of sin, our bodies become the temple of the Holy Spirit. Therefore, Paul names humans "holy," sanctified (1 Cor 6:19—"do you not know that your body is a temple of the Holy Spirit within you, which you have from God, and that you are not your own?" "For God's temple is holy, and you are that temple" 1 Cor 3:17. See also Galatians 5).

Paul's understanding of sanctity is typical. Again and again throughout the New Testament sanctity, expressed in morally (including sexually) pure lives, is the peculiar possession of the Christian, the person translated out of sin into holiness by the death of Christ and by the indwelling power of the Holy Spirit. It is in John the final prayer of Jesus for his friends on the night before he is crucified and his work finished: "sanctify them in the truth; your word is truth" (John 17:17). "In the beginning was the Word, and the word was with God, and the word was God . . . From his fullness we have all received, grace upon grace; for the law was given through Moses; grace and truth came through Jesus Christ" (John 1:1, 16-17.) Sanctity is the gift of God through the Word made flesh, the Word giving up his life for all people. Sanctity is the gift of lives made true, in that Word.

To speak, then, of the sanctity of sexual relationships in and of themselves, to "claim the blessing" for our natural inclinations and arrangements, is to impoverish the gospel. We tell a story as Christians of a great and saving love, the divine love that sees and suffers for the corruption of the good creation in all its facets and relationships, the divine love that gives its own life to put that creation right. It is a story of grace and truth: grace bringing truth to a world that has lost its way. It is a story of transformation: from sin into righteousness, from anguish to peace, from death to life. It is the word of God in Christ and in the Scriptures about the world, a word made flesh in the living and dying and rising again of Jesus, Son of God. Sanctity is the gift of this word; it is ours now by grace and not by nature.

But perhaps one might ask: why then should we not bless same-sex relationships, draw them into the sanctifying power of the Spirit so that they, like heterosexual marriage, might be made holy? If we grant that same-sex relationships do not possess sanctity as such, if we cannot claim the blessing as our due, might we not still seek it, asking God to make blessed that which shares in the corruption of creation? How are homosexual relationships different from heterosexual ones in this way? For Scripture, the problem lies in the nature of the relationship itself: the turning for love toward one's own sex is part of that distortion from which creation since the serpent has suffered. If we believe that creation, the physical world, matters—if we are not simply gnostic—then the redemption we seek as a Christian people is the restoration of creation, in the world and in each one of us.

It is not an easy answer. It asks of people whose desire is for their own sex a degree of sacrifice and suffering that heterosexual people need never know. And it asks this in a society that understands neither sacrifice nor the power of God to save. It asks it in a church that no longer has the Bible in its blood, and so is not formed and shaped by the scriptural story. It asks it in a church that struggles to live with the truth and the love that are the signs of Christian community and that make sacrificial living possible.

If the church is to ask sacrifice of homosexual people it must surely be driven to its knees in repentance and in prayer, for sacrifice is not its current style. The argument for the natural sanctity of same-sex relationships, the movement to "claim the blessing" as a right forms a narrative of the rights and virtues of the natural human that has replaced in our lives the biblical story of sin and death, and the cross of Christ. As Christians we are invited to rejoice not in our natural bless-edness, but at the amazing grace of God. We are invited to uphold each other in community in the sacrificial living that is part of God's grace, and to see in those called to sacrifice an image of the Christ. The hope . . . the promise . . . of Scripture's story is that if we dare to embrace that story, if we follow Christ, if we take up his cross, we will find it to be—against all expectation—the way of life.

NOTES

1. George Brooke, "Susanna and Paradise Regained," in *Women in the Biblical Tradition* (ed. George Brooke; Studies in Women and Religion 31; Lewiston/Queenston: E. Mellen, 1992), 92–111.

CHAPTER FOURTEEN

Reflections on Holiness: A Prayer

Lisa Wang

*Holy God, holy and mighty, holy immortal
One, have mercy upon us . . .*

*Holy, holy, holy, Lord God of hosts: heaven
and earth are full of thy glory . . .*

For thou only art holy, thou only art the Lord . . .

Lord my God, I am here before You to reflect with You on the meaning of the word "sanctity."

The first thing I realize is that another word for sanctity is "holiness."

And the next thing I realize, of which I am sure, is that *You* are holy. You are holiness.

We proclaim this in our prayers, with the ancient prayers of the church, and with the even more ancient words of Scripture. We sing with the angels and the saints, "holy, holy, holy," and with them we glimpse something of who You are. And we adore.

In this, I know that holiness is something so immense, so deep, so real, that I cannot fully grasp it. Yet I know it is one of the reasons why

I love You. Your holiness draws love from my heart like a stream whose source is not my own.

So I know: if I love God, I must love holiness.

And if I love holiness, it's not just something I admire from afar, which has nothing to do with me. If I love holiness, it will change me. It will change the things I do, and think, and feel, and say. It will change my dreams, my goals, and my desires. It will change what brings me joy, and what brings me sorrow. It will change who I want to be, what I want to be, and why.

So, loving God means loving holiness, and loving holiness has all these implications for what life means to me and how I live it. Indeed, it will leave no corner of my life untouched. For this reason I know that when people say holiness is simply "being set apart," that is clearly not all it is. If holiness is being set apart, it is being set apart *for God.* It is being *taken up* by God, for God. It is allowing ourselves to be *taken hold of* and *changed.*

I am reminded by this of the words from St. Paul's letter to the Philippians:

> But whatever was to my profit I now consider loss for the sake of Christ. What is more, I consider everything a loss compared to the surpassing greatness of knowing Christ Jesus my Lord, for whose sake I have lost all things. I consider them rubbish, that I may gain Christ and be found in him, not having a righteousness of my own that comes from the law, but that which is through faith in Christ— the righteousness that comes from God and is by faith. I want to know Christ and the power of his resurrection and the fellowship of sharing in his sufferings, becoming like him in his death, and so, somehow, to attain to the resurrection from the dead. Not that I have already obtained all this, or have already been made perfect, but I press on to take hold of that for which Christ Jesus took hold of me.

Phil 3:7–12 (NIV)

What does it mean to say, "Christ Jesus took hold of me"? And what is "that for which" He has taken hold of me? What is this thing that the apostle Paul wants so much to "press on to take hold of" that everything else seems like "rubbish" in comparison? St. John Chrysostom (c. 347–407) has said that it is nothing less than "our Life and our Salvation":

> [The Lord] saw us in such great guilt, yet did not reject us; was not angry, turned not away, hated us not, for He was a Master, and could not hate His own creation. But what does he do? As a most excellent physician, He prepares medicines of great price, and Himself tastes them first. For He Himself first followed after virtue, and thus gave it to us. And He first gave us the washing, like some antidote, and thus . . . all our guilt . . . took [its] flight at once . . . Our eyes were opened, our ears were opened, our tongue spoke holy words: our soul received strength, our body received such beauty and bloom, as it is like that he who is born a son of God should have from the grace of the Spirit; such glory as it is like that the new-born son of a king should have, nurtured in purple. Alas! How great nobility did He confer on us!

Homily 11 on Philippians[1]

To be taken hold of by Christ, said Chrysostom, is to be healed and cleansed; to have our eyes, ears, and lips opened, so that we might see, hear, and speak *holiness*; so that we might receive, "from the grace of the Spirit," "such beauty," "such glory," as that of God himself.

"Behold, I make all things new" (Rev 21:5, KJV). This is "that for which Christ Jesus took hold of me." This is why You, my Jesus, came to us and joined your life to ours in your holy incarnation. This is why You suffered, why You died, and why You rose again. You took hold of us, in your nail-pierced hands, so that You could make us your new creation.

No wonder Paul said that compared to *this*, "I consider everything a loss . . . I consider them rubbish, that I may *gain Christ* and be found in him." No wonder he said, *"I press on* to take hold of that for which Christ Jesus took hold of me."

But do *we*? This is something that Chrysostom noticed: "The Apostle hasted, that he might be near [God]. We haste, that we may be far off."[2] Jesus comes to us and offers us "the grace of the Spirit," the mercy of forgiveness, the beauty of holiness, the very glory of the only-begotten. And instead of rushing, like Paul, to take hold of all this, we chase after a "glory" of our own making, a "happiness" of our own construction. We do things that are ugly, and call it beauty. We bind ourselves, and say we are free.

But instead of making us free, said Chrysostom, "These things have destroyed us, and what is more dreadful than all, when we are in a foreign country, and feeding on husks, we say not, Let us return to our Father."[3] Unlike the repentant prodigal, and unlike Paul, we run *away* from the love of God, to embrace instead what is empty and vile. "Are not these things then worthy of lamentation?" Chrysostom exclaimed. "Are they not worthy of tears? Whither do you fly, wretched and miserable man? Whither do you fly from your Life and your Salvation?"[4]

What is it that makes us "fly" from You, Lord? Why would anyone turn away from healing to brokenness, from hope to despair, from peace to self-torment, from freedom to slavery? I think it is simply our inability to receive your love. We can't take it in. We have been "feeding on husks" because we couldn't believe there was a feast prepared for us. We even see You, running to welcome us with your arms open wide, and we think, "It's a mirage. It can't be. There is no such thing as a Love so immeasurable, so freely given, so abundant—for me." And we turn back to feed on what is slowly starving us, all because we cannot believe there is anything more than this.

O my Jesus, You have taken hold of us precisely so that we might take hold of You, the holy One, and nothing less. What an unfathomable reality! To take hold of God himself! What makes us think we could do this and then go on eating husks? What makes us think we can love You and keep on saying and doing all the old things? What makes us think that to take hold of the living God means anything less than that we will be utterly transformed in the consuming fire of your love?

For *"we all, with unveiled face, beholding as in a mirror the glory of the Lord, are being transformed into the same image from glory to glory, just as by the Spirit of the Lord"* (2 Cor 3:18, NKJV). If we truly believed this, if we even just hoped it, we would never run away from You or behave as if we didn't know You. We would never forget that your glory is our destiny, because You have had this in your Heart for us, and for all your creation, from the beginning.

> "Beloved, now we are children of God; and it has not yet been revealed what we shall be, but we know that when He is revealed, we shall be like Him, for we shall see Him as He is. And everyone who has this hope in Him purifies himself, just as He is pure."

> 1 John 3:2–3 (NKJV)

If we have "this hope" in us, why should we despair of becoming the people You have made us to be?

Why should we think, "I can never be holy," when all things are possible with You?

Why should we think, "I don't want to be holy," when You have destined us for glory?

Why should we think, "I don't need to be holy," when each day we die a little more because we turn away from You?

"Behold, I am doing a new thing; now it springs forth; do you not perceive it?" (Isa 43:9, ESV)

You have given us all things, Lord. Yet how much I need your grace to "perceive" it: to trust in You, to believe in your love, to have *this hope* in me. To say with Paul: I want to know You, and the power of your resurrection, of sharing in your suffering, becoming like You in your death—and allowing the water and blood which flowed from your side to make me alive with your Life.

My God, grant me, who am so far from being holy, the grace to *press on to take hold* of You, who are holiness itself.

Make me your new creation, for this is what it means to love You and to be loved by You.

This is holiness. And in holiness, may You be glorified forever. *Amen.*

NOTES

1. http://www.newadvent.org/fathers/230211.htm

2. Ibid.

3. Ibid.

4. Ibid.

www.ingramcontent.com/pod-product-compliance
Lightning Source LLC
Chambersburg PA
CBHW031258090426
42742CB00007B/504